The T.I.M.E. Method™

A no bullsh*t guide to creating an abundance of time

By Monique Lindner

Front cover and illustrations by Sabina Kencana
Foreword by Gregory Giagnocavo

ISBN 978-9949-7492-0-1 (Paperback Edition)
ISBN 978-9949-7492-2-5 (Ebook Edition)

Published in Estonia
First printing September 2020

Published by
Pineapples & Pirouettes Press
A publishing house under Pineapples, Pirouettes & The PowerWoman oü
Männimäe, Pudisooküla,
Kuusalu Vald,
Harju Maakond,
74626 Estonia

E-mail: news@moniquelindner.com

Visit:
https://www.moniquelindner.com or
https://thetimemethod.com

Dedication

To my beloved grandfather Hans Helmut Lindner,

who left this planet earth way too early, yet left
me with the greatest wisdom of my life:

*"Monique, you can do anything and be
anyone you want in your life!"*

So be it.

Table of Contents

Foreword

*"Time is what we want most,
but what we use worst."*

—William Penn, 1694

William Penn was one of the first to settle in what is now America, seeking religious freedom. Although that was written more than 320 years ago, sadly, it's as true today as it was then.

The use of our time for maximum productivity and to appreciate life has been the subject of many writings going back thousands of years.

So it shouldn't surprise you that one of our biggest challenges to success and optimum performance is our struggle to manage our time.

William Penn should have had this book.

Imagine if learning the lessons Monique teaches in The T.I.M.E. Method® could improve and optimize your life? To help you create time, multiply your business, and harness the power to give you more freedom.

Well, there is no need to imagine – the book is here and you have that power in your hands right now.

I've been in business for more than 25 years as a founder or co-founder of several successful businesses – from real estate development to publishing to Internet providers to emergency services to telecom. I still have an interest in the telecom company, but now spend my time consulting with companies to help them accelerate growth. In addition, I am involved in a small non-profit run by my wife, a nurse, providing health care to indigenous Mayans in Central America.

So I am no stranger to the many demands on my time.

I would imagine the same type of demands you face daily. So much to do, so much you feel you must do. Too many distractions and interruptions.

And that depressing feeling of inadequacy and disappointment when the week is over, your must-do list is only half-completed.

Time is precious and limited and yet we tend to waste it by not spending it wisely.

I'm glad You found this book.

I'm glad you have this book in hand because that makes you a member of a group of people who seek high performance, who want to optimize their time and create freedom.

A group of people who don't want to waste time. Not anymore.

In my entrepreneurial career, all but one company became a success. And my successes were thanks to the many fine, energetic people I was fortunate to associate with in each venture. One company failed despite having Microsoft, PriceWaterhouse and a wealthy investor as partners. When that happens, all you can do is lick your wounds, reset your mindset and move on. And learn from it.

You probably don't realize how important mindset is to time management and productivity. I don't think I did at that time.

Fortunately, I was able to restart my entrepreneurial engine and create a new business 18 months later. That success made up for the one that failed and reminded me that failure is temporary. And that using time wisely produces permanent results.

Yet, I do have some regrets. My (few) regrets are rooted in my inability to effectively manage my time for optimum performance. In short, I was too busy, too many late nights and weekends, for too many years. Some say I may have ADHD. I prefer to think of it as my creative side getting in the way of my to-do list.

It wasn't for lack of trying. I really did try to be more efficient, more productive.

I was diligent about buying leather-bound agendas, scheduling pads and planning boards. And they helped. A bit. I also bought and used 'executive time management systems', with sections, colored tabs and 'Do This Today' pages as well as software programs that reminded me of what was due and when.

Those things did help, even if only a little bit. To anyone else, I looked very organized carrying my leather, color-tabbed agenda with me to meetings. However, the truth was darker – I just couldn't seem to find the time to even plan effectively.

I am very proud of the companies I started, the hundreds of jobs created and the financial rewards obtained. However, I am left to wonder what if I had this book back then? I could have used 20% less energy and worked 20% fewer hours. I could have created time and life would have been so much more rewarding on a personal and family basis.

You've heard the phrase "You have as much time in a day as Beyonce". The implication is that she gets far more done in a day than you do. I haven't investigated it deeply, but I am sure that it's true.

So what is stopping me, or you, from being more efficient, more productive? From getting more done in less time? How can we 'create' time so that we have more of it so that we can enjoy life more fully? This book will help you.

I wish for you to avoid the traps of mismanagement of time. I wish for you to avoid the feelings of too much to do and not enough time. I don't want you to feel the stress that comes with realizing the day is over, you're exhausted, and the list of must-dos are still there, undone.

You need what I didn't have early on. You need the understanding that 'time management' and 'to-do' lists don't necessarily result in productivity. Let's face it, you can manage your time, scratch things off your must-do list and still not reach maximum optimization and performance.

How many times have you wondered why you're behind, when you've been so busy, worked so hard?

I believe this book will give you the answer to those important questions. I also believe that if you commit to understanding, absorbing and implementing what Monique shares, you can become super-efficient and super-productive.

The wonderful additional bonus is that you will learn how to optimize your performance without sacrificing freedom and happiness along the way.

The elements of human optimization and resilient efficiency are not completely unknown. They aren't some sort of new or recently-discovered ancient secrets. However, thanks to Monique's years of research and lived experience, they are now available to all of us.

What is new and exciting is that this book breaks down those elements so you can easily understand what she calls The T.I.M.E. Method®.

And her clear explanations of these productivity and time-creation elements make The T.I.M.E. Method® easy to implement in your personal life and your business life.

This book will be my personal go-to book to help me create time and supercharge my productivity.

I hope you will commit to implementing what you learn from this book, so that you too, will supercharge your productivity and create the time and freedom you deserve.

Thank you, Monique,

Gregory Giagnocavo

Denver, Colorado USA

Introduction

I am lying on the floor of my studio apartment, my parents beside me, every light in the house turned on. An ambulance arrives on the scene. The doctor and emergency nurses race up the stairs to my studio, rush in, and get to work immediately. I watch them set two IVs, one in each hand. I was pale, my limbs flat and motionless on the yellow carpet.

> *Wait. Why can I see myself lying there? Where am I?*
> *Why am I not reacting to the ambulance team?*

I am floating in the upper corner of my living room. Outside of my body, there is no time and space. All that remains is light.

I can see myself because my heart has stopped beating. *Do they know?*

I turn around and float towards the light. It's bright, brighter than hospital LEDs. So bright that I almost regret turning around.

Now everything around me is filled with this white light. A warm yellow glow in the distance pulls me in like a magnet.

Flashbacks of memories pop up along the way, life memories that mean nothing to me now. In one of them I am fighting with my ex-boyfriend a few months back. I watch myself furious, smashing the flowers he had given me over the front of his car.

I moved faster towards the warm yellow light. I just wanted to get away from this all. This didn't feel good.

> *How did I get here anyway? I'm only 19 years old! What the heck have I done to end up here?*

I mean… now that we're talking about it, my life wasn't all that joyful. I had been working 18-20 hours a day since I was 13 years old. I didn't have a single day off in those entire 6 years, nor would I want to. Who would I spend that time with? Myself? Pfft. No thanks. My ex-boyfriend, who would either talk down to me or else ditch me completely to party and get drunk instead? No, I had better plans: I worked. Day in and out. Oh, and there was my university, where I had to catch up on work since I had to change programs after being sexually harassed. And after my grandma died, what was the point of any of it?

> *So…maybe the question is not, "how did I get here," but, "should I stay?"*
>
> *But what would "staying here" mean? Am I dying? Because this light… I mean… am I not out of my body already?*

I see myself motionless on the floor. The IVs in my still hands pump medicine into my blood.

What about my parents? My parents, who fought for me and my life for so long, and so often. Should I leave them behind? Would anyone remember that I was ever here? Did I do anything to be remembered? Anything good...anything extraordinary?

*NO! Oh my gosh, no! No! If I die now, I will just be another number, another statistic. F*ck.*

Can I get out of here? I don't wanna be in this light. I don't want to be here.

I'm going to fight. That's what I do. THIS IS NOT MY TIME.

I turn around, away from the light. I fight with everything left inside of me, every ounce of will, every scrap of hope. Every bit of belief that I was made for something bigger.

Everything goes black.

Time is Life

Baboom.

Baboombaboom.

A pounding pain in my chest brought me back to life with the brute force of a ton of bricks. I opened my eyes. I saw that blinding light again, but this time, it was real. It was the light in my living room.

My heart started beating again. I looked around. Ambulance. My mum talking to me, my dad on the carpet beside me, holding my hand. His face, worried like never before. Lights. Noises. All of the yellow. Everything went dark again as I fainted. This was all a little too much for someone who just woken up from the dead.

I went to see my neurologist the next day, who was shocked but oddly excited. My migraines were often accompanied by epileptic seizures and we both knew the intense side effects that both conditions caused. I usually experienced intense pain in my head that felt like ongoing, throbbing, stabbing electric shocks. Some people might be tempted to call them headaches, but I promise, that is not comparable at all. They come with many other dysfunctions caused by loss of blood circulation in the brain. I often saw stars and black dots blinking in front of my eyes. I wasn't able to form words or speak in sentences. I would mistake spatial perception, falling down stairs or running into walls because I misjudged distance. These were some of the common symptoms I dealt with, on top of other typical side effects like intense nausea and vomiting, loss of consciousness, and losing the ability to function as a human. Top this off with seizures that sent muscle cramps rippling through my body. What would look like panic attacks would make my toes and fingers cramp so badly that I wouldn't be able to separate them, and my whole body would shake like a washing machine at high speed.

My neurologist and I both knew, however, that this was different. We exchanged a few words before I did an ECG and a brain scan (CT). I was sent as an emergency case to a cardiologist who performed several different tests, including a heart ECG. When I was called in for results the next day, my neurologist was again half worried and half excited.

"You were clinically dead, Monique. For about 25 seconds. You can see this here…" he pointed at the scan, "…and here. We can also see that there are chemical changes in some areas of your brain. But we don't know exactly what the impact of those changes will be."

He showed me the ECG results, the brain and heart waves with strange gaps and outliers, and went on to tell me this:

"Monique. I am fascinated by you. I am 73 years old, and in all of my 50 years of studying migraines, the brain, and neuroscience, I have never seen anyone as resilient and perseverant as you. The extreme physical pain you have already endured for so long has such a significant effect on your daily life, yet nothing can hold you back. It doesn't even seem to depress you at all. And now, you have experienced a clinical death, and it's as if this is just another day for you."

He was right. It WAS just another day for me at that point. And at that moment I realized: time is an illusion. Einstein already told us about time as an illusion long ago, and he explained it with math and science. But I mean something slightly different. Up until that day I thought I was invincible. I thought I could push myself as hard as possible, and then beyond that. So many things in my life had gone so badly. I had been sick from the day I was born. First my kidneys, then my nervous system, and then my stomach and intestines took a big hit due to all of the antibiotics. The list goes on with other rather severe diseases and injuries, yet here I was. Alive. Somehow I had made up this story in my head that nothing can kill me, that I can survive whatever comes at me. Do you know this feeling? The feeling that "that happens to other people but it will never happen to me!" Until it does. And it did.

The problem is that we think we have time. We think that we somehow "own" time for as long as we live. But we don't actually know how long that will be. So we use our time recklessly and waste it, just as we do with other resources that seem infinite, like water and food.

When people feel safe and stable, they easily slip into a false sense of invincibility. We get a cold, and then recover. We make a mistake, and after a few weeks no one talks about it anymore. We jump from bridges with nothing but a rope attached to our feet and hop out of airplanes with a tiny parachute on our backs, and for what? For fun. We risk our health for money and fame. We only wake up from our daydream bubble the day that life throws a curveball the size of a wrecking ball.

Suddenly we face a family member's death. Someone close to us is fighting cancer. We lose a dear friend, a job, or our partner. Sometimes, it is us out on the battlefield. And we suddenly wonder, "How much time do I have left?"

In a world where we are taught that "time is money," I want to tell you that's not true. Money comes and goes. We can print it, burn it, recreate it. Time is much more valuable.

Time is life.

Dying saved my life. It showed me that we are not here to waste our time with things that don't light us up, with people that don't actually love us, or working jobs that we resent.

Time is here to be lived fully.

Now I live every day I get to experience as if it was a new life. One life a day. That's all I got. That's all YOU got. It has become my mission to live with that understanding, that each day is one full life, and to be absolutely, 100% comfortable with the thought of each day being my last day ever. Because how do we know if tomorrow will ever come?

There is no need to die to be fully alive. I hope you never have to experience it. That's why I know that this book is important to you. I know we all want more time in our lives, more freedom, more intention.

On a search for more time, our quest to live "our best lives," we read blog posts about "the top 10 secrets to productivity," we read books about "The 4-Hour Workweek", we go to conferences about making more money in less time, then we come home and surprise! NOTHING EVER WORKS.

These experts say, "You are just one funnel away from living your best life!" But then that funnel doesn't work, breaks the bank, and drives you insane.

These experts also say you just need to "manifest" your next clients, but how the heck do you do that?

They did not work for you because you relied on someone else's framework, blueprint, and secrets to work in *your* life, in your business, in your daily routine … but you didn't look at it with common sense, and you didn't take any responsibility for making these blueprints your own and adapting them to YOUR life and business. You just took it "as is." Because the experts said it works. After all, you are just one (insert whatever tool/secret/product they sell) away from success, right? Not quite.

But that's exactly why I wrote this book. I'm going to show you a grand vision of what's possible. I want you to know how far you can go and what options you have to unlock your ultimate potential. I'm going to give you a variety of tools, methods, and techniques, so you can find out which ones work best for you! Take what works for you, and leave the rest as is. I want to help you strengthen your mindset and build up your confidence, resilience, and grit so that you can go at least one step further than you've ever imagined was possible.

That's the exact mindset I created The T.I.M.E. Method® with. I developed this framework over a decade of studying and working for high achievers like you. People who are tired of chasing time and craving freedom and a life of impact and intentional living.

In my pursuit to create something that anyone and everyone can work with, I found that there are 4 pillars that are fundamental to success, not just in a material or financial sense, but also a sense of lifestyle and fulfillment.

The four pillars of The T.I.M.E. Method® are:

Time Management - To create more time we have to learn how to manage the time we have. Although this is not always possible, there are many different techniques and methods to help you do it. These techniques will help you take space from the hustle and grind and business that otherwise takes over our lives. As high achievers, we always strive to do more, be more, and have more. But what if we can have it all by only doing what is necessary but with the best of intentions and highest quality?

Impactful Leadership - It's great to want it all and be it all. To do so, we need to be a person who can hold space to receive as much as we give. We need to be able to get out of our own way and to guide others to where they want to go. We need to become leaders who stand firm in our own truths, and who can inspire and influence others. This kind of leadership always starts from within.

Mindset Mastery - Many people say that the "right" mindset is what makes 90% of our success. But what does the "right" mindset look like? I believe this is a question everyone needs to answer for themselves, yet this pillar gives mechanics, methods, and guidelines that everyone can adapt and integrate in order to grow. And growth is the real recipe for success.

Energy Efficiency - We can manage our time as much as we want; if we are not efficient with our energy, we will waste our time. Energy Efficiency teaches us how to set boundaries and standards and hold ourselves as well as others to them. To keep our energy at its highest, we need to create an environment that allows us to be the best version of ourselves.

Time Management
Goal Setting
Off Days
Prioritizing
Planning
Scheduling

Impactful Leadership
Modern Leadership
Burnout Prevention
Perfectionism
Core Values
Leadership from within

Mindset Mastery
Discipline
Resilience
Factual Thinking
Crisis Management

Energy Efficiency
Detoxing
Boundaries
Habits & Routines
Focus
Intuition

If you have read other productivity or time management books, you were surely keen to implement the scheduling or planning tips, only to find out that after a couple of weeks you were exhausted yet again. That's because most other systems out there only look at one or two of these pillars. They don't acknowledge the fact that each pillar won't stand without any of the others.

We can not manage our time if we do not learn how to efficiently use our energy. We can not become an impactful leader without mastering our mindset. None of these techniques work without the others. Yet all of the systems I have seen try to sell you quick wins just to tell you (and sell you) later, "Oh, now that you are productive, you should also know that you better take care of your mind, or do you want to burn out?!"

That's why this framework is so different. I'm not here to give you more "expert advice." I don't have another blueprint or any secret steps. This framework is not another collection of blog posts, and it is also not a scientific paper. This is about real life. I am only sharing what has worked. Then you take what works and feels good for you and leave the rest behind.

This framework is adaptive. I developed The T.I.M.E. Method® over a decade-long corporate career across different positions in different countries. I incorporated my experiences being chronically ill and living with tons of pain, which robbed me of functioning, "normal" time that most people have. I had to learn how to be extremely efficient by the time I was four years old. At that age, no one had yet taught me anything about time management or efficiency, so I became creative and made up my own rules.

Each pillar of the framework represents one chapter of the book. At the end of each chapter, I will review what we learned in the form of action steps for you to implement so that you can integrate each technique straight into your life and business without wasting time or energy.

These action steps are accompanied by a virtual book experience I created for you, which you can find at www.thetimemethod. com/bookexperience. I created this virtual experience to accompany the book because I know people with different learning types have different needs. The virtual experience is for those of you who are not the greatest linguistic learners and need more visual support, as well as for those you that like a more guided learning experience.

Remember, I am not telling you to be better, do better, be more, or do more. I am bringing you back to the roots. I want you to **slow down to speed up.** That's what this book is all about. If I learned one thing in life, and if you take only one thing away from this book, it's this:

If you want to get more done, you have to do less.

Does it work every day? No. Ha! That's also an illusion. But I can promise you that if you follow the framework in this book to find your own "one life per day," you will live a fuller and richer life than ever before, and you will achieve more than you could ever imagine.

CHAPTER 2

Foundations

Two primary factors led to my cardiac arrest and clinical death: overworking myself and ignoring all warning signs that appeared in the 6 years prior. Suppressed and unprocessed trauma added a few blows to the final knockout. I didn't know about any of this at the time, and it would take me another 5 years to learn.

I didn't understand how critical sleep is to our brain and body. I didn't know that there was more to it than just your energy or your ability to think clearly. So I barely slept. Until fairly recently, just before my 33rd birthday, I slept no more than 4 hours a night, every night, for 20 years. I can still function perfectly fine with just 4 hours of sleep, but about a year ago I realized that I needed to change this habit. Even if I am *able* to sleep only 4 hours, I still *should* sleep for more. I'm working on it, and these days I get about 5 hours of uninterrupted sleep a night. That's how long it's taken me to unlearn all the things I have unconsciously forced upon myself.

In the hopes of avoiding another cardiac arrest, I started working with my amazing neurologist to learn more about the brain, as well as various body functions and different nervous systems in our body.

I quickly learned—maybe because I worked night shifts for more than 7 years—that our body works in rhythms based on daylight. I learned that if we interrupt our body clock, we can mess up everything from our physical health to our mental and emotional health. That's why it is so important to know the foundations of these functions. They are called circadian rhythms, biological clocks, and chronobiology.

Over the years, I have come to a very clear understanding of how these work for me, what it looks like when I don't honor them, when they allow me to be hyper-productive, and when I need to rest. For the last decade, this knowledge has also helped me to improve my clients' productivity dramatically while decreasing their working hours up to 50%. Based on these natural biological phenomena and experiences with my clients, I was able to identify and describe four different basic productivity types that support exactly what we are here for: getting more done by doing less. In the coming sections, I will explain these body functions in detail, outline why we need them, and show you what they have to do with creating an abundance of time.

SECTION 1| Circadian Rhythms, Biological Clocks, & Chronobiology

Our body follows different circadian rhythms, such as the light-related circadian rhythm that dictates when you sleep (at night) and when you wake up (during daylight). Circadian rhythms are physical, mental, and behavioral cycles that follow a daily clock of roughly 24 hours. Some examples are your sleep-wake cycle, the body-temperature cycle, and the daily hormone cycles, among others. Our circadian rhythms can be influenced by external circumstances such as temperature, nutrition, or time zone changes when traveling.

We also have biological clocks. Imagine these as feedback loops composed of genes and proteins. They cycle through rising and falling patterns created by the feedback between the proteins and genes. These patterns produce circadian rhythms and regulate their timing.

Finally, there's the body clock, which is scientifically called the suprachiasmatic nucleus (or the SCN), a system of over 20,000 neurons in a region of our brain called the hypothalamus.

Chronobiology is the scientific field that studies these cyclic phenomena in living organisms and their adaptation to solar and lunar rhythms. These cycles are known as biological rhythms. In simpler terms, chronobiology is the body's biological timer, defining our body temperature, our sleep rhythm, and so much more.

If you follow your own biological clock instead of chasing some trendy entrepreneurial wake-up club, your body will thank you for it in the long run (as well as your spirit and your mind). Ignoring our biological rhythms can have serious consequences. Pushing ourselves to wake up at 5 a.m. even though that's outside of our circadian rhythm can have major side effects.

a) If you aren't getting to bed early enough, you will face sleep deprivation and all of the issues it brings. See the infographic on the next page to see how sleep deprivation affects the body.

b) Even if you are getting enough sleep, forcing your chronobiology to change can impact the rest of your biological rhythms. This can cause either insomnia or fatigue as well as other issues like constant hunger or lack of appetite. These in turn can lead to further health issues like eating too much or not eating enough and hence not getting enough nutrition.

c) Your stress levels can rise due to your changed sleeping and eating schedules throwing off your body's natural melatonin and cholesterol production

These are only a few examples, but they should be enough to show you how important our biological clock really is.

memory issues

During sleep, your brain forms connections that help you process and remember new information. A lack of sleep can negatively impact both short and long-term memory.

trouble with thinking and concentration

Your concentration, creativity, and problem-solving skills aren't up to par when you don't get enough rest.

accidents

Being drowsy during the day can increase your risk for car accidents and injuries from other causes

mood changes

Sleep deprivation can make you moody, emotional, and quick-tempered. Chronic sleep deprivation can affect your mood and lead to anxiety or depression, which may escalate.

high blood pressure

If you sleep less than five hours a night, your risk for high blood pressure increases

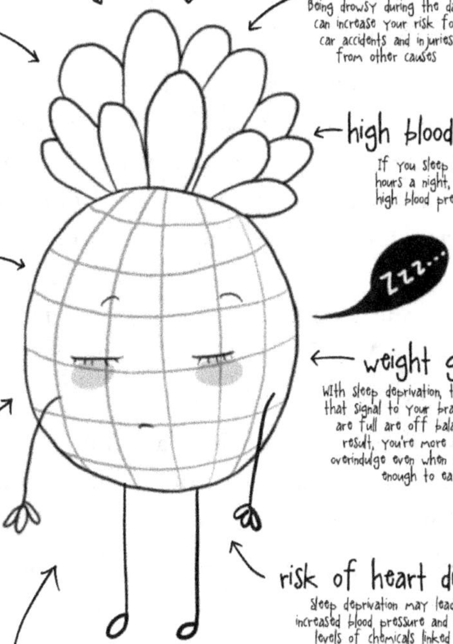

weakened immunity

Too little sleep weakens your immune system's defenses against viruses like those that cause the common cold and flu. You're more likely to get sick when you're exposed to these germs.

weight gain

With sleep deprivation, the chemicals that signal to your brain that you are full are off balance. As a result, you're more likely to overindulge even when you've had enough to eat.

risk for diabetes

Too little sleep weakens your immune system's defenses against viruses like those that cause the common cold and flu. You're more likely to get sick when you're exposed to these germs.

risk of heart disease

Sleep deprivation may lead to increased blood pressure and higher levels of chemicals linked to inflammation, both of which play roles in heart disease.

low sex drive

Too little sleep weakens your immune system's defenses against viruses like those that cause the common cold and flu. You're more likely to get sick when you're exposed to these germs.

poor balance

Lack of sleep can affect your balance and coordination, making you more prone to falls and other physical accidents

 www.moniquelindner.com

 @themoniquelindner

Different people have different chronobiologies. They all do follow a more-or-less 24-hour cycle and repeat after that, and there are broad similarities in most of the timeframes of our body clocks, but it's fair to say there is diversity. They are pretty easy to detect, too. Look at you and your parents, or your siblings, or your partner. When do you go to bed on a weekend, and at what time do you naturally wake up in comparison to the other person?

There is a good reason why I do not believe in the 5 AM Club for all entrepreneurs. I would never recommend it to a client unless their chronobiology actually works for the 5 AM Club (which is frankly quite rare). Ironically, I am a perfect candidate for the 5 AM Club, as I naturally wake up between 4:30 and 5:15 a.m., but I still don't recommend it. When used by someone whose chronobiology wants them to wake up later, the 5 AM Club can have a seriously negative impact on someone's life and wellbeing.

(As a quick side note, there are things I love about Robin Sharma's book. His notion of morning rituals is indeed very powerful.)

But what does all of this have to do with productivity?

A lot!

Depending on our natural chronobiology, there are different times of the day where our productivity is naturally higher than at other times. So if you want to get more done while working less, you need to figure out what your chronotype is and then leverage it as much as possible.

Different versions of these chronotypes exist in the science world, but I have never resonated with any of them, nor have my clients. Instead, I will share my own version of different chronobiology types that are not only based on the body clock but also the most common energy types that I found to match these particular chronobiologies. I call them the chrono-energy types.

CHRONO-ENERGY TYPES

① Sun-Chaser

TIME	ENERGY LEVEL	ACTIVITY
4:00 am – 6:00 am		Wake up happily before the sun rises
Wake up – 8:00 am		Enjoy a quiet morning watching the sunrise, sitting outside, and breathing fresh air. Take it easy and use the morning hours for spiritual work, self-care, reading, journaling, and personal time
8:00 am – 9:00 am		Shower, listen to a podcast, have tea, and get ready before the workday starts
9:00 am		Start the workday with the Most Important Task (MIT)
10:30 am		Stretch out, have another tea (or maybe a coffee), smoothie, or a fresh juice. Usually, skip breakfast
11:00 am – 1:00 pm		Another work sprint, this time with Additional Tasks (AT)
1:00 pm		Prepare & eat lunch
2:00pm – 4:00 pm		Recharge energy by taking a rest, going for a walk, hanging out on social media, or listening to a podcast
4:00 pm – 6:00 pm		Last work sprint of Secondary Tasks (ST)
6:00 pm – 8:00 pm		Make dinner. Listen to a podcast or watch masterclasses, rarely socializing or networking
8:00 pm – 10:00 pm		Wind down with journaling, energy clearing, meditation, etc.
10:30 – 11:00 pm		Go to sleep

② Morning Lover

TIME	ENERGY LEVEL	ACTIVITY
6:00 am – 7:00 am		Wake up with full energy, ready for the day
7:00 am – 9:30 am		Hit the gym, go for a run, or do a yoga or MMA session, followed by a nice shower and getting ready for the day
9:00 am – 9:30 am		Protein shake and breakfast
9:30 am		Answer emails and messages
10:00 am – 12:00 pm		Attack the Most Important Task (MIT)
12:00 pm – 1:00 pm		Prepare & eat lunch
1:00 pm – 1:30 pm		Go for a walk
2:00 pm – 2:30 pm		Answer emails, chats, messages
2:30 pm – 4:00 pm		Work Sprint of Secondary Tasks (ST)
4:00 pm – 4:30 pm		Make a smoothie, protein shake, or fresh juice and have a snack
5:00 pm – 6:30 pm		Last work sprint of Additional Tasks (AT)
6:30 pm – 8:30 pm		Cook and eat dinner, listen to podcasts or an audiobook
8:30 pm – 10:00 pm		Socialize and network, call friends, or hang out and read a book or watch a documentary
10:00 pm – 10:30 pm		Go to sleep

③ Day Cruiser

TIME	ENERGY LEVEL	ACTIVITY
8:00 am – 9:00 am		Coffee first. No words spoken before coffee!
9:00 am – 10:00 am		Read blog articles, browse social media, listen to a podcast. Another coffee. Shower and get ready.
10:00 am – 10:30 am		Breakfast. Oh, and coffee.
10:30 am		Answer emails and messages
11:00 am – 1:00 pm		Attack the Most Important Task (MIT)
1:00 pm – 1:15 pm		Coffee. Just kidding (or am I?). Have a quick snack.
1:15 pm – 3:15 pm		Work sprint of Secondary Tasks (ST)
3:15 pm – 2:30 pm		Ooops. Forgot lunch. Oh well. Another snack. And a smoothie or shake.
2:30 pm – 5:00 pm		Work sprint of more STS and Additional Tasks (ST)
5:00 pm – 7:00 pm		Cook and eat dinner
7:00 pm – 8:30 pm		Record a podcast, do an interview, write emails, messages, etc.
8:30 pm – 10:00 pm		Socialize, network, call friends, or hang out reading a book or watching a documentary
11:30 pm – 12:00 am		Go to sleep

④ Night Owl

TIME	ENERGY LEVEL	ACTIVITY
10:00 am – 11:00 am		Wake up. Music. Take it easy. Shower and getting ready first.
11:00 am – 11:30 am		Breakfast and Smoothie
11:30 am – 12:30 pm		Answer emails and messages, browse Social media, watch interviews on Youtube, or tackle the next section of an online course
12:30 pm – 1:00 pm		Quick and high-intensity workout
1:00 pm – 2:00 pm		Lunch and coffee
2:00 pm – 3:00 pm		Works on a creative passion project
3:00 pm – 5:00 pm		Begin to work here and there on Additional Tasks (AT), planning, and taking it easy
5:00 pm – 8:00 pm		Order in or meet friends for dinner
8:00 pm – 10:00 pm		Work Sprint for Secondary Tasks (ST), just getting warmed up
10:00 pm – 10:30 pm		Short break, quick social media check
10:30 pm – 2:00 am		Work on Most Important Task with bathroom and tea breaks in between
2:00 am – 3:00 am		Wait? Is it already night? (Go to sleep reluctantly)

These are the most common chrono-energy types and the activities that align with their natural cycle of energy levels. Look specifically at the time of day and the energy level depicted by the battery. Which of them feels most accurate to you? Of course, this is just a very short introduction to these archetypes and some things may feel off to you. As soon as you find which of the five chrono-energy types that rings the truest, you can figure out how to be more productive in less time, utilizing your high energy levels for the hardest tasks and the lower energy levels for low-maintenance activities or those that energize you.

What happens if we mix up our energy levels and task categories that are most suitable for those times? The quality will lack, more mistakes will be made, and it will overall take much longer for you to get the tasks done. When our brain gets tired, it looks for distractions more often than it does when its brain-mass battery is still fully charged.

So what can we do to keep our brain-mass battery full for as long as possible? How can we use our energy and chronobiology as energy and our chronobiology as best as possible?

The simple answer is to use this book. The whole thing. I'm serious, that's what it is for.

To keep your battery full for an extended time without experiencing decision fatigue after just a couple of hours, it is best to implement all (or most) of what you are about to read. In short, that means managing your time, becoming a leader who is true to themselves, mastering your mindset, and being intentional with your energy.

Remember, I made it all as simple as possible for you with a virtual book experience at www.thetimemethod.com/bookexperience.

SECTION 2| Rest / Sleep

This one is so undervalued it's insane. I was guilty of that oversight for over a decade, not sleeping or resting when I should have, and that neglect certainly caught up to me later in life. Did you know that sleep deprivation will kill you before food deprivation does? This fact alone should tell you a lot about how important sleep is. More important than food!

When we skip sleep we are not saving time. Instead, we are adding on to the many layers of sleep deprivation that can continue to grow into a wide variety of physical issues. Instead of trying to save time by skipping sleep, we can actually increase productivity and hence save time by sleeping the ideal number of hours for our body, which differs from person to person.

As you can see there's a big misunderstanding about sleep and rest: It is not just to recharge your body and regain energy (though this is part of it). Sleep is the single most important activity you can do to keep your brain healthy. During sleep, two different types of brain cells perform a cleaning process to get rid of toxins, prune synapses that the brain doesn't need anymore, and repair the brain's neural pathways. If you are not getting enough rest, even though you may not feel sleep-deprived, you are taking away the opportunity and essential time for your brain to recover and detox what has been accumulated as clutter throughout the day. And in doing so you increase your risk of Alzheimer's disease, diabetes, cardiovascular diseases, and obesity.

Are these risks worth an hour or two of skipped sleep a day? I promise you, they are not. And before you think, "well, that's not gonna be me. I can sleep just 4 hours and I am okay," then think again. Think about the people you know with these kinds of diseases. What do they have in common? Maybe not enough or restful sleep? Maybe stress? Maybe something else? One thing is clear: if you ask them to choose between the disease and one or two hours more sleep per day, there's no question which one they'd choose (spoiler: it's the sleep.)

So what should we do about sleep? There is only one correct answer: Don't cut it. But what does that really mean? I'll get you started on the basics, and I also recommend my fellow author Shawn Stevenson's book, *Sleep Smarter*, an excellent introductory guide to all things sleep.

I like to ask the sleep question from this perspective: Who are you? What are your needs? What are your circadian rhythms, biological clocks, and other physical conditions that determine your sleep? This is a great time to have a look at your chrono-energy type that we have previously established and compare if your sleeping times fit into that type. Do they differ? If so why?

Sometimes we do not get the sleep we need for many different reasons, and that is a great indicator to start exploring what you can do to improve your sleep. If your sleep patterns are feeling great for you but you feel like your energy levels throughout the day don't match your current work style, see what comes up when you look at your chrono-energy type. For example: just because we like going to the gym in the morning doesn't mean it is the best option for our energy levels and productivity. So when you combine your sleep patterns and energy levels, check what comes up for you and see where improvements are the easiest to implement, then go from there.

In general, scientists say that a healthy adult needs between 7-9 hours of sleep daily. But that is not true for everyone. Even more important than quantity is the quality of your sleep. Are you getting through the 4 stages of sleep properly, is it taking you too long to fall asleep, are you waking up at night, are you getting enough REM and deep sleep… These are the most important components of quality sleep, but to write about this here would take us away from our actual mission, and other people like Shawn are better resources for this topic.

The message here is clear: Don't cut corners. Better said: sleep! Or it'll kick your ass later.

SECTION 3| Productivity Types

Next up are what I like to call "productivity types," or the different quirks and work styles that seem to work better for different kinds of people. Similar to our chrono-energy types, we all have different ways of focusing and concentrating on tasks. Some people can get into highly focused work quickly but can lose focus just as fast. Other people need a bit longer to get into the groove of a task but can stay focused for a while. Once you have determined your chrono-energy type, you are one step closer to figuring out which productivity type you are best suited for. These two factors together will ultimately help you to leverage your most productive times.

In this section, I'll lay out a few different methods of working productively. I will mention these again throughout the book, but I'm going through them here because I want you to know that you have a choice.

No, you don't have to work with Pomodoro if it's not for you.

Yes, there are different work styles for people who have trouble focusing on a single task for longer than 5 minutes.

Yes, there are also work styles for people who love to lose themselves in work for hours at a time. It's all in here.

The different productivity types are described in order, from the shortest amount of time spent on a task to the highest, and include a description of the kind of people for whom each style works best.

5 MINUTE SNIPPETS

I developed this technique to help my clients with ADHD work in a way that's more appropriate for their needs.. They've struggled with other methods because they simply can't keep their focus on a single task. They would forget what they were doing, chase the next shiny object, and then end up frustrated and defeated because they didn't get their tasks done, or they had to work much longer hours to do so.

→ **Who is this for?**

This work type is best for people with a very short attention span and people who are easily distracted. It is designed to give your mind space to wander in between focusing on tasks, instead of suppressing the need and then not being able to focus because all you can think about is the thing you are trying to suppress. (This, by the way, is a scientifically-proven psychological trick with a great name: The White Polar Bear Phenomenon or Ironic Process Theory. It says that the more you consciously try to suppress a certain thought, the more likely it is to surface. For example: Try not to think about dancing pineapples! ...See?!)

It is also great for people with ADHD / ADD, for whom long sprints of work are a huge challenge and a source of more suffering than productivity.

→ **How does it work?**

1. Clear your desk of everything except a glass of water and your laptop (or whatever you are working on) on the desk.

2. Take the tasks that you would like to work on and break them down into 5-minute snippets.

3. Each of the tasks that you want to tackle shouldn't take longer than 1 hour in total to accomplish.

4. Broken down into five-minute snippets, each task should take a maximum of 12 snippets to complete.

5. Once you've broken all the tasks down, plan them throughout the first part of your day

6. Prepare a timer so you can time two different things: the 5-minute task snippets, and the time you allow your mind to wander in between. I usually recommend giving it just one or two minutes max.

Over time you will notice that you can increase your time working on tasks. You'll go from 5 minutes up to 7, then 10, and later on you may even be able to train yourself up to the next productivity type.

POMODORO

This technique was developed by Francesco Cirillo in the late 1980s. It is based on the famous little tomato timer you may know from your kitchen. The Pomodoro technique is a work cycle that loops between short stretches of work and breaks, either 25/5 or 45/15, to help stay productive and create a tangible timeline for small goals or deadlines.

→ Who is this for?

This is best for people who are not very organized, get easily distracted, and need more structure during their days. It works very well for admin tasks, or any type of tasks that do not require you to think deeply into structures and formulas (like web/app/AI development) or ideas (like writing).

→ How does it work?

https://www.tomatotimers.com/

1. Prepare your desk with only the things you need for the task and a glass of water

2. Pick a task to work on and set a tangible goal for the first Pomodoro set

3. Set your timer for 25 minutes (you can also find a Pomodoro timer online)

4. Remove all possible distractions

5. Start working on the task

6. As soon the timer is over - take a 5-minute break

7. During the break, I highly recommend not sitting in front of a screen, but move, stretch, have a little healthy snack, drink water, sing, dance, or whatever is fun for you and energizes you. Messages, Facebook/Instagram and any other work or brain-washing activities are not on the list for breaks ;)

8. Repeat these cycles 4 times (that's a total of 2 hours)

9. Take a 30minute break after that

10. Restart the second cycle

This is the traditional Pomodoro set & cycle set up. There are different variations, which can be useful if you work a 6-hour workday, for example, instead of a full 9-hour day.

WORKSPRINTS

Worksprints are similar to the pomodoro technique, in that they are a set up of work and break cycles. With worksprints, the time spent working is longer than it is with pomodoros. The breaks are longer as well, so I like to pre-plan what will happen on a break, because it is easy to fall into a "let me just quickly check social media" kind of mood, and that is exactly what we want to get away from.

→ **Who is this for?**

These worksprints are perfect for the last part of a morning routine, so you can knock the most important task out of the park before lunch. It is for people who can sit through work for 90 - 120min. without getting easily distracted, or that need the time to think deeper about the task at hand. I often suggest this type for developers, writers, creatives, and anyone building automations or systems, for example. The longer stretch of time allows you to ease into the right mindset and get lost in the task without interruption, without taking you all the way down a rabbit hole.

→ **How does it work?**

Worksprints have 2 components that work together: the work cycle and the break cycle. They complement each other if set up correctly.

1. Prepare your desk with only the things you need to work. If get hungry easily, prepare some healthy snacks (like veggie sticks or nuts) and have a glass or bottle of water on hand to stay hydrated

2. Choose a task for the first worksprint. I recommend starting with the most important task (MIT).

3. Set a goal for what you want to achieve during the sprint.

4. Plan your break cycle: For the first one, I usually recommend movement and breathing. This can be a walk outside, it can be stretching or yoga, or it can just be getting up and moving in whatever way feels best for you.

5. Set your work timer. I recommend setting it for anywhere between 90 to 120 minutes.

6. Set your break timer so you can immediately switch after your sprint. For a 90-minute work sprint, I recommend taking a 15-minute break. For a 120-minute work sprint, I recommend taking a 30 min break.

7. After your first cycle, repeat for a second one, but make the second break a long one, like an hour. Take this time for lunch, a walk, a work-out, or anything else that energizes you

FLOW STATE

What most of my clients strive for and what so many of us are looking for: the Flow State. For many people, it's a mystery how to achieve it at all. The term was popularized by positive psychologists Mihaly Csikszentmihalyi and Jeanne Nakamura to describe the mental state one achieves when fully immersed in an activity or work for the sake of the activity or the work itself. In flow state, a person experiences such joy or satisfaction that they lose track of time. They are focused exclusively on that activity and can not be easily distracted. Feelings or distractions like hunger, mind chatter, pain or aches from sitting, fatigue, or exhaustion simply do not surface in a state of flow.

→ **Who is this for?**

The flow state is for people who want to challenge themselves to uplevel their focus, discipline, and work ethic. Since it is a mental state it differs from the other productivity types in how it is achieved. There are many books on this topic, but I wanted to give you a few simple steps that can help you set yourself up for successfully achieving flow state.

→ **How does it work?**

Flow state knows no time. People who step into flow state lose all sense of time and can easily work a 4-hour sprint without getting distracted or needing to move or change tasks. That's why your setup is super important, as you want to maintain your physical and energetic state at the highest possible level. These steps are a simplified version to get you started and help prepare your body, mind, and spirit for flow state.

1. Be prepared - Know that once you reach flow state you will probably forget time. So being prepared is the #1 rule. That means having enough water (and I mean 2 or 3 liters of water to keep you hydrated throughout the entire flow state) and healthy snacks that support the brain like nuts, veggie sticks, avocado, and so on. Make sure to sit or stand in a comfortable and healthy position so that a stiff neck or inflamed shoulder muscles don't knock you out of flow state.

2. Stay calm - Mind chatter is the enemy of focus. Avoid it by setting yourself up for a calm state of mind. If that

means you need to meditate before you work, do so. If you need to do a heavy workout to clear your mind, then that's what you need to do. Whatever it is that clears your mind, eg. a run, dancing and singing out loud, a cold shower, journaling, do that!

3. Clear all distractions - This is one of the most important yet overlooked steps. So many people are afraid to turn their phones or notifications off, put their devices into airplane mode, tell their kids to stay out of the room and ask their partner to take care of them, and so on and so forth. You may read this and think "yeah, this is easy to say when no one needs to call you and you don't have kids." Yep. But what can I say, that's all a choice. Plus, no one said you have to do this every day. This is the part where you have to decide how much you want this, and then take 100% self-responsibility for that choice. You gotta stick it through if you really want to make it happen.

   In this case, less is more - Less clutter on your desk. Fewer things in your room or office to look at and make your mind wander (like photos of family, etc. the more minimalistic, the better). Remove all devices that you don't need from the room, and put the one you are working on in airplane mode or, if you need the internet to work, use a blocker for social media and websites other than the one you use for work. Make it as hard as possible for yourself and your brain to cheat.

4. Schedule your distractions - When you're making your calendar for a day in flow state, write down or plan the afternoon for your wandering mind, shiny object hunting, chatting, Facebook stalking, and Instagram story posting. This is the key to getting it off your mind. Instead of trying

to suppress it, make time for it—intentionally. That means you plan to do all of these distracting things AFTER you are finished working. Make sure you write it down. It is a physical and psychological reinforcement for your brain that it does not need to remember to be distracted.

5. Don't force it - Flow state is a mental state. Just like meditation, it may or may not work on your first try. It may look just like what you read about in books, or it might look very different for you. You might slip into flow state super fast, or it might take you what seems like forever to get there. Take it easy. Be kind to yourself. Don't push it. Keep practicing and make sure to know when to step out and when it's time to step in again.

# CHAPTER REVIEW

This chapter has provided the foundations that we will use throughout the rest of the book. These are some of the primary tools we need in order to implement the other skills we will learn in the coming chapters. Take this knowledge about your chrono-energy type, your productivity type, and the importance of sleep, and keep it in mind. It will help you move the needle farther in the direction of more time and get you closer to unlocking your ultimate potential.

To help you review what we have learned in this chapter, I have put together a few action steps for you:

1| Visit www.thetimemethod.com/bookexperience and sign up for your virtual book experience.

You'll find all the exercises in this book and tasks laid out there as well as all of the rest of the resources I am sharing, laid out in an easy and accessible way. I may add some other bonuses along the way, you never know.

2| Find out what your chronotype is.

There are a lot of different ways of doing so. There are online tests you can take, but I have found that most of these are not very accurate. In your virtual book experience account, you will find a resource that explains the 4 different chronotypes, what they mean, and their characteristics based on the typical circadian rhythms these chronotypes follow. You may not fully resonate with any of them, or you might resonate with two of them a little bit, and that's fine. More importantly, assess yourself. Pay attention to yourself, noting when you get tired, when you wake up (without an alarm), when you feel hungry, and so on. Follow the tasks in your account to assess yourself, and find a conclusion that way.

3| Figure out which productivity type is the best fit for you.

I recommend trying each of them out for a week to see if you get more quality work done than before. If one of them feels off for some reason, don't force yourself into it.

Time Management

Over the years I have redefined time management for myself and for my clients over and over again.

Growing up in Germany, "time management" basically meant to be better, faster, harder, stronger. In the corporate world it mostly meant to complete the same amount of work in 8 hours that other people usually get done in a week (yes, that's a thing. And yes, I did that. And no, I can not recommend it). You could basically schedule your own burnout for 3-5 years down the line of working with that high intensity.

As a semi-professional ballerina, time management for me (especially between the ages of 3 and 13) meant to go straight from school to arrive at training right on time, five times a week. It meant being able to do all my homework and somehow also get in enough practice time at home, often all while in constant and intense pain.

As a daughter and little sister, time management meant to squeeze my chores at home into the schedule, being on time for meals and taking part in all family activities while bringing great results home from school.

In school, time management meant doing my homework during class or during breaks while other kids played because the rest of my days were regularly filled with agony (migraines, blurry vision, auras, vomiting, and kidney or urinary tract infections were often waiting just around the corner). So juggling class and homework plus socializing with the other kids was managing my time as a kid.

As a chronically ill kid, time management looked like running from one doctor's appointment to the next to find out what was wrong with me. Then, when I finally got a diagnosis after 5 long years, it meant going back to that doctor to find a possible treatment or relief.

All of this time management also meant that sometimes, walking home after school, I would sneak away into the park to play in the little stream, climb trees, collect bugs, and just hang out alone in nature. I wanted to get away from all these duties, and along the way I would forget the time until... uh, my parents would have to search for me, ready to call the police until I showed up, just in time, after hours of playing.

Today, time management means freedom. It means that when I manage my time, I can control it. That I can make the most out of my time, without being a slave to it. It also means that I can create my life exactly the way I want. Because if you manage your time wisely, you can fill it with all the things that bring you joy, the fun things you love doing, and the things that fulfill you, all while making all the money you'd love to make.

I learned to live by the concept of "Alive Time versus Dead Time" before I even knew to call it by those names, coined by my all-time favorite author Robert Greene. According to Robert Greene, the difference between the two is the difference between a life lived with pride and one lived according to others' expectations and filled with things that make us miserable.

Dead Time, in this case, describes the time we spend waiting for things to happen to us, working for others but not on our own dreams, and doing things to impress people, fulfill other people's expectations, validate ourselves and juggle whatever else comes our way.

Alive Time is the time that we are in complete control of. We are not waiting for things to happen to us, but rather deciding what happens to us (as much as is possible) and choosing how to react to what happens outside of our control. A life full of Alive Time is a life lived fully, all while learning and growing.

But what does this look like in real time?

Robert Greene once said, "The worst thing in life you can have is a job that you hate, that you have no energy in, that you're not creative with and you're not thinking of the future. To me, might as well be dead."

I am not recommending immediately quitting your job. But I resonate highly with what Robert Greene is saying. Without consciously knowing it or having heard of this concept at the time, this is exactly what I was doing for all my professional life.

In most of my jobs, I had horrible bosses and team managers, except for one operations manager who was an incredible leader and another CEO who was a great manager. But most of the other bosses I worked for drained my energy and sucked all the joy for the job out of me.

Instead of being miserable, I decided to turn the inevitable dead time into alive time. I used the dead time to join a leadership certification program and gain more expertise. I took the time to get to know my team on a personal level. I also took the time to observe other team leaders and managers around me, studying the team's reactions and how that influenced their results.

Over the last decade, all of that work and experience has helped me develop the framework of The T.I.M.E. Method®. In hindsight, I am so grateful for the challenge of dead time because it gave me the chance to be productive and learn. The opportunity to transform dead time into alive time is what brought me to where I am today.

So how does this apply to you? Look at your life and ask yourself:

Are you stuck in a job you hate? → How can you use the time at this job to improve your skills, expand your knowledge, or develop yourself?

Are you in a relationship that makes you feel miserable? → How can you use this time to learn more about yourself and safely transition out of the relationship?

Do you feel anxious or depressed? → What is it that makes you feel this way? How can you take control of it? What would it take to change it step by step?

If you can look at what makes you feel stuck/unhappy/miserable/depressed/anxious/bored etc. and ask, "What would it take to get out of this situation?", then you can take back control and move forwards step by step.

Once you start moving forwards you are already one step closer to using your time wisely. This is where time management comes in. I know many people, including most of my clients, feel pressured and overwhelmed by the thought of time management. That's because they think of time management as a chore, "another thing you have to do."

But what if, instead of a chore, you could see time management a technique that you can internalize to help you to live life fully, just like breathing is a technique for your body to get oxygen and stay alive? What if you didn't have to force yourself to do it? There are ways to practice time management in a more supportive way that doesn't make it feel so damn hard and icky. In reality, time management is pretty dope.

Before I lay it on you, I want to make sure we are not misunderstanding each other. Time management by itself is a broad topic. It's huge. If you'd ask me on any given day to tell you something about time management, I could talk for 72 hours straight without having to repeat anything. Since I totally understand that it can feel a bit unapproachable, I have broken it down for you from big-picture goal setting, moving through prioritizing, into planning, and finally down to the granular level of daily scheduling. I am covering each of these topics in their own section so that you can follow along and take what works for you and leave the rest.

That is the way time management works for me. We want to keep it as simple as possible. In the end, you decide what is worth your time, and that is what time management is really all about.

Time management is the result of the decisions you make about what is important to you and hence deserves your time.

SECTION 1| Goal Setting

WE LOVE GOALS! Right? Yeah, but did you know that there are hundreds of ways to set goals? As with everything, we hear all about the most common goal-setting methods, but that doesn't mean those are always suitable for us. Many high achievers don't know when or how to use the different goal-setting methods available to them. Let's bring some clarity to the confusion.

In this section, I'll show you different methods for setting goals across different time spans. What good is it if we have 15 methods for setting short-term goals but we have no idea how to plan for our long-term goals? When we set goals for different phases and time spans of our life, (for example 1 year, 5 years, 10 years, etc.), we can align the direction of each of our shorter-term goals and actions with the next-longest time frame as our biggest and longest-term goals. Not everyone needs goals that are planned for 15 years ahead, but if you have extremely big dreams for yourself and you know you are here to fulfill a mission, I'd recommend taking a shot at it.

I will cover four different methods: Legacy Goals, Empire Goals, and Lifestyle Goals, as well as the better-known S.M.A.R.T. Goals.

Legacy Goals are lifetime goals, planned for the next 15 years or more. You may be shocked to hear this, but there are plenty of people who love to plan this far ahead and for whom this method works extremely well. These goals include all areas of our life and business and will give an overview of what you are aiming to achieve in your lifespan.

Empire Goals are planned for a span of 10 years or more and are focused on the business side of things. The intention is to create a long-term goal for your business and answer questions that will keep you going in the right direction and help you make decisions along the way.

Lifestyle Goals are meant to help you dream up every sensory detail of your life for the next 5 to 10 years. They are all about the way you want to be living, what this will look like, and how it will make you feel. These can get into the smallest specifics and help you really visualize the future ahead of you.

S.M.A.R.T. Goals are the most popular of all of them and they should be a planning method that everyone uses at least in their business. S.M.A.R.T. Goals are perfect for planning out shorter-term goals, from 3 months to 1 year. They are designed to be very specific, which sets you up for accountability and structure on the way to success.

Just as all four types of goals have different functions and intentions, so too do we use different methods to set them. Now we'll look closer at the methods and processes.

→ LEGACY GOALS (lifetime, 15+ years)

I am not sure that many people are even aware of what I call "legacy goals" or "empire goals" (I talk about empire goals in the next step). I talk with my clients about legacy goals in a way that is fun. It is important to be able to look far into your future and know what you want, but without the pressure of expecting the outcome to look EXACTLY that way.

Legacy goals are lifetime goals, goals that will take more than 15 years to accomplish, and there's a good reason not to get fixed on the exact outcome. Say your lifetime goal is to have $15 million in your savings account at all times, run a successful non-profit, live in a Mediterranean country in a beautiful house close to the ocean, and work just 3 hours a day while maintaining your favorite hobby and an amazing, supportive partnership.

While this little blurb is a great elevator pitch to your future, it is not as inspiring as it could be. It sounds nice, but it's not the head-in-the-clouds cinematic vision that will really make you reach and dream. It's not picturesque enough to make you taste it. It's still too abstract to make you really, truly feel it.

Your legacy goal is a combination of your empire and your lifestyle goals, which we will talk about in the next two steps. We are not planning legacy goals out on a granular level but rather setting intentions and directions for where we would like to end up in our life. And when we start identifying, planning out, and working towards these goals, we can achieve them even sooner.

Take time to sit down and think through what you really want in *all* of the areas of your life, in addition to business. Here are the 7 main categories that I found to be most meaningful in our lives. They are listed in no particular order here, but you can prioritize them if you wish:

1| Lifestyle

2| Business

3| Partnership

4| Health and Wellness

5| Wealth

6| Mind

7| Spirit and Impact

I highly recommend setting up a one-pager for each of these categories. On top of each one-pager, include a photo or graphic that expresses the sentiment of what you are about to write out. Then, in the body of the one-pager, write out a paragraph or two in response to each of the following 5 questions.

a)   What is your ultimate moonshot goal for this area?

b)   Why is it so important to you?

c)   How will it make you feel to achieve this goal? What will it change for you and the generations to come?

d)   Who is your biggest inspiration for achieving this goal? Who are you looking up to?

e)   How committed are you to achieving this goal? How much do you really want it? What are you willing to do for it?

If you feel like adding anything else to the one-pager, please do so. This exercise comes from a place that is very dear to our hearts, so any comments or keywords that will help you remember where you are heading should go in the notes section at the end. If you like to use our worksheet for this exercise, just head over to www.thetimemethod.com/bookexperience.

We are not writing any deadlines here because legacy goals can take a lifetime to achieve but, as mentioned above, can also materialize faster than we anticipate. While our idol may have spent 20 years achieving similar goals, we may only need 13. Time can be a restricting construct if we use it to limit ourselves. If we leave the timeline open, we can achieve more in a shorter period than we might believe is even possible.

Now, what are we going to do with these one-pagers?

Keep them close! Read them out loud once a week. I believe strongly in the power of reinforcement. We are familiar with this concept when it comes to training dogs, for example, rewarding them with snacks when they do something right like sit down on command. But we don't use it often enough for ourselves!

Reinforcement works in different ways. In this case, we use visual and verbal reinforcement by reading our goals and speaking them out loud. Hearing our own voice is powerful. Our brain builds stronger connections to ideas, instructions, and thoughts when we hear them in our own voice. This is a big reason why affirmations can work so well.

A very powerful way to build neural pathways (the bridges that connect information in our brain) is to record each of the one-pagers as a voice note and listen to them. You can do so each night before you go to bed, or as part of your morning routine, or, if you would rather do it less often, after your weekly planning session on Sundays (more about this later on). These are just suggestions, but the reinforcing power of repeatedly reading and listening to your goals will help you believe in and achieve them.

→ **EMPIRE GOALS (10+ years)**

Empire goals can be seen as a 10-year business plan that will merge into your legacy goals. I am not asking you to write out an actual business plan. What we will do instead is answer a checklist of questions. These can be answered in bullet points, graphics, or written paragraphs and detailed plans—whatever format works best for you as a direction and a guideline to follow.

These questions are based on the work we will be doing throughout the book and on The T.I.M.E. Method® framework and principles.

a) What product/service are you selling and how does it stand out in the market?

b) What is your vision, and what is your mission for your business?

c) Who are your customers?

d) How are you changing their lives?

e) How are you different from your peers in the market (not the product or service but you or your brand)?

f) Other than not being able to keep the business alive, what would be the worst-case scenario that could happen in the first 10 years? Write it out in all detail.

g) How can you prevent the worst-case scenario before it occurs?

h) How can you solve the worst-case scenario, should it occur in any form?

i) What does success look like in the first 10 years? This should be both tangible and intangible. Even though success is often measured monetarily, it can also be (and hopefully will be for you) a feeling like confidence or pride. Who can you ask for support or feedback? This question is for when times are rough and as well as when things are through the roof, because in both of these times our minds play tricks on us. It will be important to have people to support you through both of these phases, to cheer you up when you're down and cheer you on when you're successful, without a doubt of jealousy or ill intentions.

j)   What does your team structure look like? Where will you find the right people, how will you attract them to work with you, and how will you empower them to do their best possible work with joy and enthusiasm?

There are many more questions to ask, especially if you are writing a business plan, but these are the ones I recommend answering for your Empire Goals. For each of the questions, take notes of resources you found, the research you conduct, and any other material you want to come back to, like inspirational people to follow, books to read, or podcast episodes to listen to. You will end up with an amazing little workbook to use while building your empire, full of the information you need to make your dream come true.

→ LIFESTYLE GOALS (5-10 years)

Lifestyle goals are probably my favorite, simply because you can dream so big and wild ... and then go and make it happen. As the name says, these are all about your lifestyle, answering questions like: Where do you want to live, and how does it look? What does it smell like, feel like, sound like? What country do you want to live in? Will you have one country as a home base and travel from there, or stay put in a huge plot of land with tons of animals? When we look at these kinds of goals we also want to look at what you are doing with your time, your money, and with whom you are sharing your time. The time frame for lifestyle goals is about 5 -10 years.

I have two exercises to help you to distinguish between 5- and 10-year goals: vision boards and "daily life" visualizations.

→ **Vision Boards - a visual action plan**

Vision boards are probably the exercise with the most resistance from many of my clients. They also generate huge numbers of people who decide to wait for luck to drop out of the sky instead. Disclaimer: this is an exercise, and as with every exercise there is an action component. The action is not the creation of the vision board but rather the intentional work you put behind it.

Vision boards look very different for different people. A vision board can be an actual board where you pin pictures and photos of your lifestyle goals. It can be a collage of pictures, photos, text, paintings, and magazine cutouts to create a sweeping creative image of your lifestyle goals. It can be a digital collage, a screen saver, a journal filled with creativity, and so on. There are no limits, except that it should be very visual and that it should be as in-your-face as possible on a daily basis.

Many people love to make vision boards but ignore the action part that comes next. That's where the following 3 questions come into play:

a)   How can you achieve this goal?

b)   What do you have to get out of the way to achieve it?

c)   Who do you have to become?

To keep the board as visual as possible, I recommend answering these questions in bullet points or just a few words if you can. You can write on the board itself or print the answers out and add them to the collage. If you are creating a journal as your vision board, you do have some more space to write should you need a few more words.

For best outcomes, look at the board every day. Then start to remove the obstacles that you think are currently in your way. Sometimes these hurdles aren't as big as we think they are, and sometimes they're not even really in our way at all. .

The vision board is the perfect exercise for your 5-year lifestyle goals. You can add all the things you envision yourself achieving in the next 5 years in one place. When we see these goals daily, it is reinforcement for our brain and we do work towards it, even unconsciously. Reinforcement is truly a powerful concept once we understand how it works.

We use a different exercise for our 10-year lifestyle goals. It is similar to one of the exercises we have done before, but we will go deeper. The exercise is called "Your Perfect Daily Life"

→ Your Perfect Daily Life

This exercise is another written visualization, but instead of going through a series of questions we will answer only one. We will answer this one question for a few stages of your life. The question is this:

"What should your daily life, an ideal average day, look like in 1 year, 5 years, and 10 years?"

Write out your answer using as much detail as possible. And I mean the minute-by-minute of your day.

Write out what your perfect day will look like at that time in your life. Start from when you wake up—what you see, hear, smell? What you do, how you feel, who is there (or not there), and what you will do? Explain this step by step. Write about the house you live in, the environment, the things you do, what you eat, where it comes from, and how it tastes.

Yes, this sounds like writing a book about your future life. You can be very concise yet precise,

or you can go on and on about all of the colors, smells, tastes, etc. too. The most important thing is that when you read it out loud you can imagine it.

Once you have written all 3 versions of it, I urge you to record it. One by one. We keep going back to the power of reinforcement and why I love it so much. I promise I wouldn't have gotten to where I am today if it wasn't for me talking to myself out loud and repeating the things I want to achieve over and over again. I have accomplished so many things that I am proud of that I simply should have not been able to do, due to, for example, physical issues like my nervous system disorder, yet I did it anyway… and I killed it.

Listen regularly to the most pressing version. So start with listening to the 1-year version whenever possible. On a commute, when you are cooking, when you are waiting for something. If you listen to it while you sleep, your subconscious mind will soak it up as important information and build strong neural pathways with it. It is so important that we feed our brain only very important information that we want to keep and grow in our minds. As the brain prunes what has not been fed, it will build up and strengthen what has been entertained, especially in the last hour before bed.

→ S.M.A.R.T. GOALS (1-3 years)

We fail to reach most of our goals because they are not specific enough, or we lose track of accountability, or the goals simply get lost along the way.

The best example is also our favorite: New Year's resolutions. Did you know that 80% of us fall off the wagon after only 30 days and a mere 8% of people actually achieve their resolutions by the end of the year? Let's look at another popular goal: yearly revenue goals. We want to hit the million-dollar mark this year! YAY. But did we make it? Probably not.

What's wrong with all of these goals and resolutions? For starters, we could say they are not specific enough. We should also notice that there is no deadline, which makes our brain more likely to take its time instead of achieving the goal in a specific timeframe. We could also point out that the goals are not very clear, and that there is no "how" mentioned at all. And we seem to be missing the accountability factor too, right?

In other words, we could simply say they are not S.M.A.R.T. goals.

S.M.A.R.T. goals (first named by George T. Doran) have been around for quite a while. In business, they are especially helpful as they give a framework for setting goals that can be taken further into planning and scheduling processes, which together make up the steps it takes to achieve your goals.

S.M.A.R.T. stands for

Specific

Measurable

Achievable

Relevant

Timebound

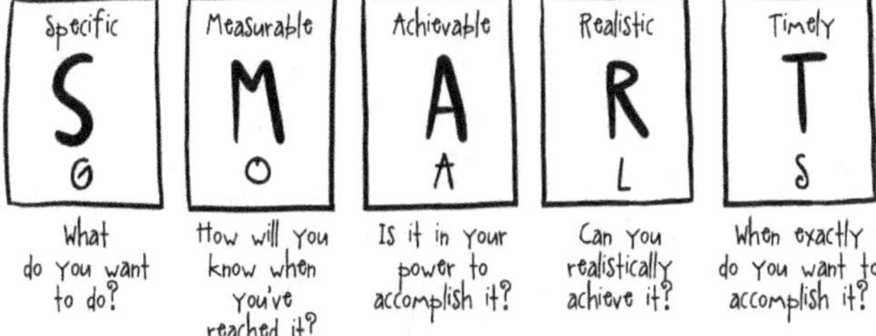

 www.moniquelindner.com  @themoniquelindner

You can already see that "I want to be healthier" or "I want to make a million dollars" does not fit into these 5 indicators. Here is what they look like when we break them down even further.

SPECIFIC

Being specific with your goal has several advantages, the most obvious being that you know exactly where you want to go. Let's take this "I want to be healthier" goal. I mean, tell me what that is. Healthier. Does that mean you eat one cow less per year? Or will you drink 2 fewer beers a day? Or is it actually saying that you now want to exercise outside 3x per week, eat vegan, completely eliminate processed foods and sugar, and only drink coffee before lunchtime?

You can see the huge range of possible answers I might get if I ask, "What does 'healthier' look like for you?" So defining your goal clearly is first and also the most important aspect of being "specific."

When you know what, exactly and specifically, you want to achieve, it automatically determines specific action steps you need to take.

If you just say you want to be healthier but there is no particular result you are striving for, then really, what steps will you take to get there? One day you might be satisfied that you didn't eat the 5 candies you'd usually eat, but the next you're hitting the gym hard without eating at all. I may be exaggerating here, but you can imagine that this is absolutely possible without clear guidance on what getting to your goal looks like.

Finally, being specific has a very clear psychological advantage. Uncertainty is a cause for fear, but certainty is a cause for action. When you have a vague goal, you have no clear steps to take towards it and you are left in uncertainty. This uncertainty can cause fear, and common reactions include overthinking, analysis paralysis… everything *except* action. When we know what to do, even if it seems scary, we take action, though sometimes that action looks more counterproductive, let's be honest! Knowing *which* steps to take will help you stick to the plan and get you more excited about it day by day.

MEASURABLE

This one gets right at the psychology of how humans achieve goals. See, the actual joy is found, not in achievement, but in the progress along the way. Don't get me wrong, hitting a goal is amazing. But if you ask the 8% who actually stick it through to achieve a New Year Resolution about their experience, the answer "I loved the progress" will most likely come up somewhere, too. This is because we are neuroscientifically hardwired for progress. Dopamine is the neurotransmitter that is responsible for feeling rewarded and motivated as well as for joy, pleasure, and even body movement. The so-called "dopamine hit" can be addictive. This is what Instagram likes, sugar, and addictive substances all have something in common: they all stimulate our brains to release dopamine. Instagram likes do not have the same physical effect like sugar and addictive substances, but if your brain feels rewarded by that engagement, it will release dopamine just the same.

Having measurable goals also helps to support the first step, being specific. If you have specific goals with specific action steps, and you can measure your progress, then you can change direction easily and quickly if needed. This saves you from making big mistakes if you look at the data regularly. Which brings us to the next step.

ACHIEVABLE

Having achievable goals is extremely important. Look, I am all about "shooting for the moon." But if you currently make $10k/ month and your goal is to be making a million per month 3 months from now, without any existing opportunities or deals pointing to this epic income increase, you may as well prepare to be disappointed. So shoot for the moon! And then build a solid rocket to make your moon landing happen. And I'll tell you what: Oftentimes, when we set goals properly, plan and structure them, and then really go for it, we achieve them much faster as we planned for.

The other benefit of having achievable goals is that it becomes much easier to enroll other people in your vision. You do not have to share your moonshot goal with them right away, but your 1-year goal may excite them, and they might want to work for you happily ever after, or for however long. The same is true for investors. Sure, they want to know where you can take a company in the long run and the big visions you want to accomplish, as obviously they want to see what's in it for them. But first and foremost, they want to know that what you are setting out to achieve is clearly laid out and doable so that the money they invest is in good hands.

RELEVANT

I feel like I am talking about something super obvious again, so please don't roll your eyes at me. Before I started writing this book, I thought, "oh, high-performers will know all this already, so I can jump right into the crazy advanced stuff that I do with my clients." But then I remembered that even with my clients, I start exactly here: with the foundations. Not so much what they are, but how to apply them. These foundations never stop being relevant. If you lose sight of the foundations, you not only leave plenty of money on the table, but you also screw yourself over in regards to time, sanity, and resources. It's an uphill battle without the foundations.

So what has relevance got to do with this? Simple. If you set goals that have nothing to do with your long-term vision, or if you set them because society tells us "high performers have to achieve these kinds of goals," or anything like this, you simply will not follow through. The relevance of a goal also determines its importance to you, and this will determine whether or not it is a priority. And as we know, we should only schedule our priorities and not just prioritize our schedule!

TIMEBOUND

It feels a little ironic, in a book all about how to create more time, to talk about why your goals should be, well... timebound. But I'll do it, because I just love talking about it (you may have noticed that already). In a 1955 article for The Economist, C. Northcote Parkinson described what's now known as "Parkinson's Law," explaining that the human brain will always fill time and space to use all available resources. What do I mean by that? Let's say you are supposed to finish a task that will take you about 5 hours of work in total, and you have a week's time to do so. Most people who are not highly organized and disciplined (so almost all of us, right?) will finish the task within the deadline but just by the end of it. If you have only 3 days to finish the task, you will also make it before the deadline, but just right before it. Now if you had only 12 hours to get it done, most people would also be able to make the deadline - usually right before the 12 hours are up.

Our brain has the tendency to use all the time we have, filling it up with activities, thoughts, and patterns because it hates boredom. It absolutely resents it. So much so that it would rather stress you out and keep you extra busy than to strategically use time and help you rest and relax in between. So we need to trick it. With deadlines.

Now that you know what S.M.A.R.T. stands for, let's go through a few examples so we know how to implement and use this system:

HEALTH

So let's say our overall goal is to be healthier this year. We agreed that this means something completely different to each of us, so let's see what this might look like as a S.M.A.R.T. goal:

By July 31st, 2020 I will eat freshly-cooked, non-processed food 80% of the time, exercise or move at least 3 times a week for a minimum of 30 minutes, and drink more than 2.5 liters of water a day as a habit that is integrated into my lifestyle.

It is **specific** because it shows you what to do (cook a certain kind of food 80% of the time, drink more than 2.5L of water per day, exercise 3 times a week)

It is **measurable** because you can calculate each of its components. Let's say you eat twice per day. That's 14 meals per week, which means at least 11 of these meals should be freshly-cooked, non-processed meals. You can count if you worked out 3 times per week for a minimum of 30 minutes as well, as well as whether or not you drank a minimum of 2.5L of water per day.

It's **achievable** because you can use techniques like meal prepping to save time, keep a full water bottle always in front of you with a reminder to drink a big sip, and schedule workouts into your calendar.

It's **relevant** because all of these new tasks can be turned into habits. This makes it easier to keep doing them in the long run and help you with your overall, long-term goal of "being healthier."

It's **timebound** because your goal is to have these 3 habits down and implemented by July 31st. You can take it step by step and address overwhelm upfront.

See how this looks so much more actionable and clear already? For the next examples, I will only put the S.M.A.R.T. letters next to the part of the goal they correspond to. and I'd love for you to explain the correlation yourself. Here we go:

WEALTH

Let's make a wealth goal, since this is what many of us are interested in. It is important to know where we currently stand financially in order to be able to set a new wealth goal. Let's say our business currently makes $750k/year in revenue selling a certain digital product. Here is our new goal:

By December 01, 2020 (T) I will make $1.5mill/year revenue (S) by hiring 3 new team members (M/A), increasing our ad spend to $50k/year (M/A) and adding 2 more products to the shop (M/A) (=R).

An expansive yet achievable goal that includes the way to get there with measurable, tangible steps, each of which is a little milestone towards the specific end goal. That's how we will make it happen!

Now let's look at a less tangible example, like relationships, whether romantic or platonic. For the sake of a clear example, let's go with friendships.

FRIENDSHIPS/NETWORK

By November 27, 2020 (T) I will add 3 new people to my circle (S) with whom I can build a great friendship, support each other in life and business, meet regularly (M/A) by going to networking events with interesting topics or like-minded people at least once a week (M/A), and put in mutual effort to follow up on our first meeting. (R)

The key with intangible goals like these is to define the indicators. That means: what does "meeting regularly" look like for you? What are the interesting topics you'd like to discuss? How do you define "like-minded" people?

Make sure you are defining these indicators so you can be really clear on what you are looking for, e.g. in a new friend, so you can set boundaries and standards around it.

Practicing the S.M.A.R.T. Goal method is going to be most helpful in your daily practice, alongside the following method we will cover next. They will help you achieve your immediate and short term goals while getting you closer to your long-term and life goals step by step, all without overwhelming you or burning you out.

SECTION 2| Off Days

Now that we have our goals, let's create an action plan for how to achieve them. The best place to start is with your days off. Yes. All the vacations you plan to take, all the bank holidays, weekends, and other days you want to reserve for celebrations, time for yourself, rest, and adventures.

Most if not all people teach it the other way around. Set your goals, plan and schedule your work, then see what is left over for you. Wow. That is not why I created my business. In fact, I plan my combined time off first, then add passion projects like volunteering and any other time I want to spend outside of my business. Only then do I know exactly how much time I have to spend on my business. This process also determines how much I have to delegate, outsource, or slim down on tasks so that I can move the needle and be more focused.

Prioritizing off days is the first huge step to shift the paradigm in your perception of time. It's like saving money. Let's say you have a monthly savings goal that you'd like to achieve. The sure-fire way to do so is to put that money aside first, as soon as you are paid, before you pay any bills, buy food, pay rent, etc. Some people may say this is dangerous. What if there is no money left by the end of the month? But this can't be true, because it is in your savings account. It's just about budgeting what you have after putting your savings aside.

The exact same system can be applied to time, with an amazing outcome. Not only will you have way more time off, adventures, celebrations, and free time, but you will also now be able to get all of your tasks done in less time. This will take practice, and you will need to apply the methods and techniques I am sharing with you in this book. But once you get the hang of it, you will have created a savings account of time.

You may be wondering about how much time off you should plan… and what if you don't know yet when you want to go on vacation? No worries. Let's start by making a list of all the off days so we can calculate them for the next 12 months.

Add all of the weekly days off to the list, and block them in your calendar, too. I highly suggest that everyone set at least one fixed day off. This can be any day. I like to take Wednesdays or Thursdays off. They fall in the middle of the work week and I can use them to relax, rest, do something fun, and go visit places that would be too crowded on a weekend.

What I don't do is use my days off for household chores. This is extremely important. You want to use your days off for pure joy, unless you love household chores so much that they relax you and you feel rested after you finish, which is a hard no from me. Quite the opposite, actually. I definitely dislike household chores, and the idea of doing them weighs so much on my energy that I hire a regular house cleaner. This is an extremely huge support for me, and it also helps support my community by hiring local business owners. So it is a win-win.

Now that you've set a fixed day or two per week to take off, you can start adding bank holidays that you will definitely want to take off and celebrate. Christmas or New Year's Eve are good examples, which might be important to you and your family. Add all of these to your list and in your calendar.

After that think about all of the celebrations like birthday parties, weddings, and events that you were invited to and want to join. Choose the ones that are non-negotiable for you and add them to the list and your calendar.

Now we've got a lot of time off already scheduled in your calendar. YAY. Next up is your actual vacation time, holidays, adventures, retreats - whatever you wish to plan. Ask yourself what would be the ideal month or season to go on holiday, and if that is on a regular basis. Make sure to write down the minimum amount of time off per year that you want to take off work and just have fun. Put it on the list. It is not as important to block out the exact dates in your calendar just yet, unless you know them already. But you definitely want to block out the number of days or weeks that you want to be on vacation.

Alright. Now that all of this is done, look at it without any judgment. Take the 365 days of the year and subtract all of the time off you just put on the list, including weekends, bank holidays, vacation time, and everything else, and see what is left. Don't be shocked or surprised. Whatever number you get is absolutely okay.

Let's calculate an example now so we have a number to work with together.

Say out we decide to take off two days a week, plus 90 days of holidays on top. Subtracted from 365 days, that gives us 171 total work days in a year. On average, that's 14.25 days per month, or 3.5 days per week. Going forward, we will calculate using these averages, though you may end up working 6 days a week for three months, and then take a full month off, and repeat. No matter what your real schedule looks like, you can use this system to create your own version based on your actual 12-month plan. For simplicity's sake, I will split the 171 days up equally.

Now we know the exact amount of time you will be using for work—171 days a year, 14.25 days a month, 3.5 days per week—let's call this your focus fund.

SECTION 3| Prioritizing

Now that you've got your focus fund set up, we need to prioritize first and foremost where we will spend our time. Since we already set our goals and then broke them down into 90-day milestones, we can now use these to create priorities.

Before we can plan anything, we need to prioritize our goals and action steps. Let's look at the tools we have to work with and how we can combine them to get the best results.

THE EISENHOWER BOX

This productivity matrix was originally set up by the 34th president of the United States, Dwight D. Eisenhower. He set up and used this matrix way before his two terms as president so that he could maximize his productivity. Besides having a full work schedule and ongoing to-do lists, he was still able to follow his passions such as playing golf and painting with oil.

The Eisenhower Box is a very simple but effective tool. As you can see in the image, it is split in 4 smaller boxes that create a grid to help you decide on your priorities.

These are the 4 categories of the Eisenhower Box:

1. Urgent and important (Do)

2. Important, but not urgent (Decide/Schedule)

3. Urgent, but not important (Delegate)

4. Neither urgent nor important (Eliminate)

To be able to use it effectively, let's look at the 4 categories and what they mean to you.

THE EISENHOWER BOX

	URGENT	NOT URGENT
IMPORTANT	**DO** Do it now.	**DECIDE** Schedule a time to do it.
NOT IMPORTANT	**DELEGATE** Who can do it for you?	**DELETE** Eliminate it.

"What is important is seldom urgent and what is urgent is seldom important."
— Dwight Eusebgiwer, 34th President of the United States

 www.moniquelindner.com

 @themoniquelindner

1. **Urgent and Important (Do)**

Category 1 is the one that will always be priority number one and also the one that needs immediate action. Whatever is in this section of the box will determine your most important tasks for the day, week, and month.

Most people think that these should be clients' tasks since your clients pay you money, but I disagree with this. Those tasks will not move your business forward, and they won't help you grow. Instead, look at your goals, mission, and values and ask yourself, "what is the number one task that will bring me closest to my goal, fastest, and with the least amount of effort?"

If you are a creative or a writer of any kind then your work should revolve around the creation of new content.

If you are a coach, consultant, healer, or work in a service-type environment, then your most important task should revolve around advancing your services and systems and marketing your business.

If you are selling products, then your most important tasks will usually be related to sales and marketing as well as product innovation.

The work that is the most important is not the one that keeps your business "afloat," but the work that moves it forward, strengthens it, and builds it up.

2. **Important, but not Urgent (Decide/Schedule)**

The "keeping you afloat" work such as client tasks, product fulfillment, coaching sessions, etc. are in category 2. Just because we are putting them into category 2 doesn't mean they are not important. They are very important, require your attention and high-quality efforts. Yet these are also the tasks that need to be scheduled.

It is crucial to understand that the difference between category 1 and 2 is urgency. Category 1 tasks are non-negotiable daily tasks. They might look different from day to day or from week to week, but they will always help you move toward your goals and keep your mission in mind.

Category 2 tasks are fulfillment tasks and are not urgent even though your clients may try to tell you otherwise. This needs proper expectation-setting which we will talk about at greater length in Chapter 6. It is important to effectively plan and schedule the tasks in this category, which we will do in the sections to follow.

3. Urgent, but not Important (Delegate)

The urgent but unimportant tasks in category 3 are often things we do to keep ourselves busy. These are very easy to outsource and sometimes we don't even have to do them at all, because they don't move the needle or make any difference to our business.

The first example of these kinds of tasks that comes to my mind is all things social media. I don't necessarily mean content creation, because there is definitely a benefit to doing this yourself, but I mean tasks like repurposing, scheduling, posting, growing channels, making graphics, video editing, and so on.

The same can be said about technical tasks, your website, anything related to software, membership sites, emails, travel arrangements, appointment making, conference booking, arranging speaking gigs, and so on…

If you look on your task list, I bet we'll find that at least 50% of them are outsourceable - yes, I am making that a word. Even though it would need some preparation like setting up workflows, processes, and putting systems in place, it's doable.

I urge you to be very honest and cut as many of these from your list as possible to free up time.

4. **Neither Urgent nor Important (Eliminate)**

This is my favorite category because we can get really honest about which of our tasks have performed poorly or not at all, or maybe we just have them on our list to stay busy. As soon as we find them, we can eliminate them.

Honestly, this is the most enjoyable part of the matrix, although my clients seem not to enjoy it as much as I do. They get rather anxious about the number of tasks I am wiping off their lists, but as soon they realize how much less work they have to do, while the results stay the same, they understand the whole notion of why I call them bullsh*t tasks.

The tasks in this category are often the ones you do when you are procrastinating from the hard and uncomfortable tasks. These are the ones that you fall back on when you don't know what to do, but they don't bring you any results. They may not even have anything to do with your business, and they don't bring any extra value to your life.

I can think of re-organizing your kitchen for the fifth time in two months. Also, discussing, sharing, and commenting on social media without a strategy or call to action. Spending endless hours researching a new idea or product even though you secretly made up your mind already. Re-designing your website, again.

For me, choosing what to eat every day, twice a day, became a big hassle. Now, instead, I plan out what to buy once a week or every couple of days, and then I just mix up a few different versions of those ingredients. I eliminated food choice from my bullsh*t tasks!

Once you've got all of your tasks (monthly, weekly, and daily recurring, as well as the less frequent ones) prioritized, you can go ahead and plan them out.

THE TRAFFIC LIGHT METHOD

If the Eisenhower Box is not your style or seems a little too overdone for you, there is a simpler way to prioritize tasks. I recommend this version to people who are already fairly practiced at prioritizing, who know what they need to do to get to their goal, and want a pretty straightforward method. This tool is an easy and simple way to do a fast assessment of what needs to be done first.

The Traffic Light is more about urgency than importance. When we use this tool, we are assuming that unimportant and non-urgent tasks have already been delegated and eliminated, and all leftover tasks are important. If you used the Eisenhower Box before the Traffic Light, then bring only category 1 and 2 tasks into this prioritizing exercise.

The colors of the traffic light indicate the following:

Red - to be done today

Yellow - to be done tomorrow

Green - to be done within the week

This is a perfect tool for your weekly task list after you have already prioritized it to make sure there are no bullsh*t tasks left on the list. Grouped and prioritized into these categories, we can now easily identify the order in which we want to work on tasks, based on their urgency.

2 STRIKES RULE

If you are having a hard time deciding whether or not a task is important, if it should be delegated, or if you should even keep pursuing it, then the "2 Strikes Rule" I developed for my clients will help you identify this easier.

The 2 Strikes Rule is very easy to use as it is just two questions. If you answer "no" to both, then the task is out, and you delete it. If you answer "yes" to both, then the task is high-priority and should be done immediately or scheduled for the same day/week.

For the best results, choose a particular time frame to look at, like the upcoming week you are planning out. Ask yourself these two questions:

1| Does this task make me money?

2| Does this task give me time back?

We already spoke about what happens if both answers are "yes" or "no." But what if just one of them is a "yes"?

Look at the urgency of the task. If the task will make you money, but won't give you time back, then it would be comparable to category 2 of the Eisenhower Box. Schedule it for later in the week, leaving enough time to finish it before the deadline, if there is one. If the task will give you time back but doesn't directly make you more money, then do it after you have fulfilled the most important task of the day, at the time of the day when you are most productive, based on your chronobiology and energy type.

THE SSP - STUPID SIMPLE PRIORITIZATION

To simplify all of these methods and give you an easy-to-adapt version of prioritization, I created my own method. There are 3 categories of the Stupid Simple Prioritization method, each of which includes all of the different priority levels from the other three methods. The Eisenhower Box model does have a 4th category, but because these represent tasks to delete, we will not work with these any further.

Category 1 is for our Most Important Tasks (MIT). These would be the "important and urgent" tasks in the Eisenhower Box, the red category in the Traffic Light system, and a double "yes" using the 2 Strikes Rule.

Category 2 is for our Secondary tasks (ST). In the Eisenhower Box, these are the "important and not urgent" tasks; in the Traffic Light these are yellow, and in the Two Strikes Rule they give you a "yes" to money but "no" to time.

Category 3 is for our Additional Tasks (AT). These are the "urgent but not important" tasks in the Eisenhower Box, the green tasks in the Traffic Light, and the "yes to time, no to money" tasks under the 2 Strikes Rule.

To make the stupid simple even simpler, here's a table to compare them.

CATEGORY/ PRIORITIZATION METHOD	THE SSP	Eisenhower Box	Traffic Light	2 Strikes Rule
Category 1	Most Important Tasks	important and urgent	Red	Yes & Yes
Category 2	Secondary Tasks	important and not urgent	Yellow	Yes = Money No = Time
Category 3	Additional Tasks	urgent but not important	Green	Yes = Time No = Money

SECTION 4| Planning

Planning and Scheduling, the next two sections, are the most important sections of this chapter. Once you get these right, the rest will work like a charm, as a lot of decision making and overthinking will fall off your plate. I'll share my favorite way to plan, which goes hand in hand with everything we have done above. The fastest way to actually implement the following planning methods indeed is when you have set a goal and prioritized what's on your list. If you skipped the exercises for the last sections, I urge you to go back and do them before reading on or to go online to your virtual book experience at www.thetimemethod.com/bookexperience to follow the steps later on in one swoosh.

Whatever your preferred way is, let's plan out your goals, shall we?

→ 3-MONTH MILESTONES

"If you fail to plan, you are planning to fail!" Benjamin Franklin's wisdom highlights the importance of planning, which is especially crucial in business. Yet he failed to mention that planning longer than 3 months ahead is a waste of time. Think about it, what happened 3 months ago that you planned for or expected? And what about 6 months ago, or even a year? Life changes fast, and I'm willing to bet things look different now than you expected. Time seems always to be running away from us, but this is just the perspective of people who fail to plan accordingly and hence waste time on unnecessary things. We are not one of these people anymore! Planning for 3 months at a time lets us look ahead a reasonable distance and stay on course, while still allowing us to periodically review our actions and change direction if necessary.

In order to make and follow an action plan with daily tasks for 3 months, we first need to know what the milestone is. What do we want to achieve in that time? Milestones mark a new chapter of your business. They are significant achievements along the way to reaching your goal. Just as a highway has regular mileage markers, the milestones we set for our business are regular markers that keep us on track and moving in the direction of our goal. To make it as simple as possible, our milestones are set for 3 months, or 90 days. Thus, there are 3 milestones along the way to our end goal, which is the 4th and final milestone.

To figure out our 3-month milestones, we will reverse engineer our previously-set S.M.A.R.T. goal, breaking it down into individual, achievable steps. Reverse engineering is the process of taking an end product (in our case we take our S.M.A.R.T. goal) and working "backwards" to unpack the steps needed to achieve this goal. "Backward" in this case means that we start with the end goal in mind and work from the goal back to the beginning. This sounds a little more complicated than it is. Here's how we do it.

1| Take your S.M.A.R.T. goal:

Write & self-publish a book by December 01, 2021 and sell a minimum of 100 copies by the launch date.

2| Write a list of the rough steps it will take to achieve this goal:

- *Create the book cover*

- *Write the book*

- *Register the book for publishing (ISBN & press registry)*

- *Promote the book*

- *Edit the book*

3| Bring the steps into the chronological order in which they must be fulfilled:

- *Write the book*

- *Edit the book*

- *Create the book cover*

- *Register the book for publishing (ISBN & Press registry)*

- *Promote the book*

4| Calculate a rough timeline each step and assign them to the respective 3-month time frame during which they will need to be completed:

- *Write the book - Month 1-3 or quarter 1*
- *Edit the book - Month 3-6 or quarter 2*
- *Create the book cover - Month 3-6 or quarter 2*
- *Register the book for publishing (ISBN & Press registry) - Month 6-9 or quarter 3*
- *Promote the book - Month 9-12 or quarter 4*

5| Create your milestones based on the previous calculation:

Milestone 1: Write the book

Milestone 2: Edit the book & create the book cover

Milestone 3: Register the book for publishing

Milestone 4: Promote and sell the book

Reverse engineering will also help us break these milestones even further until we have a granular outline of action steps that we can schedule out into daily tasks. This process, once we fully understand and integrate it, is not only simple but extremely valuable for any of our work. You can use it to break down anything, from goals to systems and workflows, or even the mechanics of a product to understand its success. Understanding reverse engineering and learning it so it becomes second nature will be extremely helpful in all areas of your business and your life.

For now, we will focus on planning. Now that we've identified our 3-month milestones, we want to break them down further into action steps and plan out each month in detail. Though we assigned 4 milestones, we agreed to only plan out 3 months ahead of time, so we will start with our first milestone, or our first three months. Once we reach this milestone, we can review our actions, recognize possible mistakes, or change track and adjust direction if necessary.

→ 1-MONTH ROADMAP

Just like in the process before, we will now break down Milestone 1 into a detailed list of action steps. This is the path we need to follow in order to achieve our milestones and ultimately our S.M.A.R.T. goal.

To do this, we will create two different points of achievement for us to keep track of: monthly targets and focus topics.

Monthly targets, similar to our milestones, are significant points of achievement along the way to the respective milestone. These are smaller highlights, planned on a monthly basis. They are the result of breaking down our 3-month milestone into 3 separate monthly targets.

Weekly focus topics are therefore the result of monthly targets broken down into 4 parts and planned throughout the month. The focus topics are the smallest units of achievement that we will plan. These will help us to determine the exact action steps we need to follow each week.

As we go through the exercise, you will realize that 3-month milestones, monthly targets, and weekly focus topics all have the same function. They just work on a different level of detail. The function is to set a point of achievement along the way, partly so that we do not lose track and also so we can celebrate wins in between major goals in order to stay motivated to keep going. Imagine having to work for one whole year without any reward, in a world of information overload and shiny objects, where everyone is seeking short-term gratification rather than long-term rewards.

These points of achievements along the way are all here for your short-term gratification, the win we all need to keep going and the dopamine-hit that keeps us running. If you want to set yourself up for success, follow this process to break down your goals into 3-month milestones, monthly targets, and weekly focus topics, and then start working your way up to the goal!

Alright, let's start setting our monthly targets for Milestone 1. We will use the same example as above, the book, so you can follow the complete process throughout the section.

CREATING MONTHLY TARGETS

1| Take your Milestone 1 that you assigned in the previous exercise

Milestone 1: Write the book

2| Write a list of steps it takes to achieve this milestone, for example:

- *Start writing chapter by chapter, starting with the easiest*

- *Combine topics into umbrella groups (these will be your chapters)*

- *Create headlines for chapters*

- *Write topics of interest*

- *Create outline*

- *Create title of the book*

- *Write introduction*

3| Bring the steps into chronological order:

- *Write topics of interest*

- *Combine topics into umbrella groups (these will be your chapters)*

- *Create outline*

- *Start writing chapter by chapter, starting with the easiest*

- *Create headlines for chapters*

- *Write introduction*

- *Create title of the book*

4| Calculate a rough timing for these steps and assign them to the respective monthly time frame in which they will need to be worked on:

- *Write topics of interest - month 1*

- *Combine topics into umbrella groups (will be your chapters) - month 1*

- *Create outline - month 1*

- *Start writing out chapter by chapter, start with the easiest - month 1 & 2*

- *Create headlines for chapters - month 3*

- *Write introduction - month 3*

- *Create title of the book - month 3*

5| Create your monthly targets based on the previous calculation, for example:

Month 1: Write out & combine topics, finish outline, start writing

Month 2: Finish writing the book

Month 3: Write the introduction, create chapter headlines, create book title

As you can see, this planning exercise can feel unrealistic for a project like writing a book. Maybe writing the book will take much longer than 3 months, and that is totally okay. The goal here is to create a tangible plan with action steps to follow. This example is just for you to understand how to approach this. A milestone can be in quarter 2 but you have to start in quarter 1 to achieve it. This could be true for writing a book. You could start writing in January and be done by May, for example.

It's most important that you understand the process of breaking big goals down to their smallest possible action steps. Don't get hung up on the details of this example and whether or not it is actually possible to write a book in 3 months(hint: it is, but don't ask me about it).

CREATING WEEKLY FOCUS TOPICS

By now I'm sure you understand how to reverse engineer a S.M.A.R.T. goal backward into a daily action plan by breaking down each of the bigger steps into smaller actions. To complete this process, we will do one final round of breaking our monthly points of achievement down into weekly focus topics. This time we will take our Month 1 target that we just assigned and break it down further.

1| Take the Month 1 target that you assigned in the previous exercise:

Month 1: Write out & combine topics, finish outline, start writing

2| Write a list of steps it takes to achieve this monthly target:

- *Bring chapters into logical order & create outline*

- *Research anything you need to know to be able to confidently write about*

- *Create umbrella categories and write headlines - these will become chapters*

- *Start writing out chapters, starting with the easiest*

3| Bring the steps into chronological order:

- *Create umbrella categories and write headlines - these will become chapters*

- *Bring chapters into logical order & create outline*

- *Research anything you need to know to be able to confidently write about*

- *Start writing out chapters, starting with the easiest*

4| Calculate a rough timing for these steps & assign them to the respective monthly time frame in which they will need to be worked on:

- *Create umbrella categories and write headlines - these will become chapters - Week 1*

- *Bring chapters into logical order & create outline - Week 1*

- *Research anything you need to know to be able to confidently write about - Week 2*

- *Start writing out chapters, starting with the easiest - Week 3 & 4*

5| Create your weekly focus topics based on the previous calculation:

Week 1: Create chapters and book outline

Week 2: Research all additional knowledge for book topics

Week 3: Write first chapter

Week 4: Write second chapter

If you look back through this section you will notice that the steps we have taken are the same for each level. The only difference is the level of detail or size of the action steps we have been able to break each goal down to. With every level, they get smaller and hence more achievable.

The very last step is to create our task lists for our weekly focus topics. This will be a little different than the breakdown we have used for the previous steps. Here is what we will do:

1| Take the 4 focus topics from Month 1:

Week 1: Create chapters and book outline

Week 2: Research all additional knowledge for book topics

Week 3: Write first chapter

Week 4: Write second chapter

2| For each of the focus topics, write a list of tasks that need to be finished in order to accomplish the weekly focus topics, for example:

Week 1: Create topics, chapter headlines and book outline

- *Make a list of topics you are interested in writing about*

- *Check which topics belong to one bigger issue - choose these*

- *Combine similar topics into umbrella categories*

- *Put topics under umbrella category in logical or chronological order*

- *Create umbrella categories and write headlines - these will become chapters*

- *Bring chapters in logical order & create outline*

- *Week 2: Research all additional knowledge for book topics*

- *Mark topics that you are not fully confident with*

- *Write out questions to answer in your research*

- *Start researching and finding valuable & credible information*

- *Collect information, list sources & citations on a resource list*

Week 3: Write first chapter

- *Choose the easiest chapter to start with*

- *Write bullet points of thoughts you want to include*

- *Bring in logical or chronological order*

- *Start writing, don't edit*

- *Keep going*

Week 4: Write second chapter

- *Choose the second-easiest chapter to write about*

- *Write bullet points of thoughts you want to include*

- *Bring in logical or chronological order*

- *Start writing, don't edit*

- *Keep going*

Can you see how this untangles more and more into actual tasks and daily action steps? YEAH. That's exactly where we want to go. At this point, we already have a pretty amazing plan for what we need to do in a week.

I would bet that these are not the only tasks on your to-do list, so this is the time when you need to add all other tasks to the list that you think you need to get done during this time. And now, prioritize as much as you can. Remember, we have different methods of prioritizing. Choose whichever one you prefer; it really doesn't matter. What matters is that you do prioritize and that you keep your focus topic and monthly target in mind when you do.

Now that you have a reasonable task list to work on, we are moving on to creating a project plan for the month. This will show you how your days and weeks are filled for the next 4 weeks. Keep on going, we are almost there!

→ THE PROJECT PLAN

For the planning nerds here, the upcoming part will be fun. In this example, we will plan out a single month. If you like to plan a little farther ahead than that, this is also an opportunity to take everything that we did above and create a plan for your whole first quarter (milestone 1). That means you will need to repeat the steps in the 1-Month Roadmap for months 2 and 3 before going any further.

In order to create our project plan, we need to allocate realistic and doable time slots for all of the tasks we have listed under our weekly focus topics, including buffer times for any unexpected interruptions.

Ask yourself how long it will take you or your team members to complete any of the tasks, including thinking it through, strategizing it, working on it, consulting with the team about it (if available), making decisions, working on changes, and then finalizing the task. For some tasks this can be done in hours. For others it will take days.

Make sure to include buffer time into your planning process. Buffer time is extremely important for accurate planning, as most tasks will take longer than you think. People get sick, feedback may not be returned as fast as you hoped or calculated, and sometimes emergency tasks come up that need immediate attention.

Over the past 17 years in this field I have come up with a very simple and straightforward rule to calculate buffer time:

- For internal tasks, where you and your team are the only ones involved, add a full day of buffer time to each work week (5 days of work).

- For external tasks, where clients or suppliers are involved, add an extra 3 days of buffer time to each work week.

The real secret is in the communication of these deadlines. For internal projects, clearly communicate deadlines *without* buffer times, to make sure the team stays on track. The buffer time will help you, as the leader, to keep the project on track should there be unexpected interruptions.

For any other projects involving 3rd party companies like clients, always communicate deadlines for work delivery *with* buffer time, so they will expect the delivery later than might be possible. When this communication strategy is combined with giving your internal team a deadline without buffer times, it gives you the chance to over-deliver to your clients, with high quality AND early or on-time delivery, each and every time.

For 3rd party companies like suppliers, communicate deadlines without buffer times, so they deliver to you in time for your internal or client-facing deadlines.

Using this rule-of-thumb kept me from turning in projects late for 17 years. Many people fear that clients will be mad or unsatisfied if you tell them a longer project scope than they want to hear. In the service industry we have become used to the expectation that everything be done right now and delivered immediately. But this is absolutely impossible, unless you're at a nail studio or hair salon, and even then you often have to wait for a free chair.

It is incredibly important to learn how to set expectations with clients and customers. This will give you the ability to set the project up for success, not only by delivering on time but also by delivering on expectations and quality.

Let's continue to use writing a book as our example. Because we are showing how buffer days work, they will be added here. This might be the case if we were writing a book for someone else, or if someone (like our editor or publisher) was waiting for us to finish the book by a certain date.

WEEK	TASK	INTERNAL DAYS	+BUFFER DAYS
1	*Make a list of topics you are interested in writing about*	1	
	Check which topics belong to one bigger issue - choose these	0.5	
	Combine similar topics into umbrella categories	0.5	
	Put topics under umbrella category in logical or chronological order	0.5	
	Create umbrella categories and write headlines - these will become chapters	0.5	
	Bring chapters into logical order & create outline	1	Total +1

2	*Mark topics that you are not fully confident with*	0.25	
	Write out questions to answer in your research	0.75	
	Start researching and finding valuable & credible information	3	
	Collect information, list sources & citations on a resource list	1	Total +1
3	*Choose the easiest chapter to start with*	0.25	
	Write bullet points of thoughts you want to include	0.5	
	Bring into logical or chronological order	0.25	
	Start writing, don't edit	3	
	Keep going	1	Total +1
4	*Choose the second-easiest chapter to write about*	0.25	
	Write bullet points of thoughts you want to include	0.5	
	Bring into logical or chronological order	0.25	
	Start writing, don't edit	3	
	Keep going	1	Total +1
TOTAL		**19**	**4**

As you can see, we have added 1 buffer day for every 5 working days. We only added 1 buffer day because we are not working with suppliers or 3rd parties here. All of the work is on our plate.

Planned work days are in the "internal days" column, followed by the calculated buffer times. This means that there are 19 total work days involved in accomplishing this monthly target. You might immediately recognize an issue here. The focus fund that we calculated only has a total of 14.25 work days in a month.

How do we fit 19 work days into 14.25 available work days? We don't. There are two options.

1. If you are working with a team, then it is possible to handle 19 days worth of tasks within 14.25 work days. Some of the tasks you have planned could be done by different people at the same time. Other tasks will be able to be fulfilled faster, and still others will only take half the calculated time if two people work on it together.

2. If you are working alone, plan the project out over 2 (or possibly 3) months. That just extends the timeline, but doesn't change the target.

Once we have allocated times to each step, added buffer times, and re-assessed our timeline for the project, we are now ready to set up the project plan.

The easiest way to set up a project plan is to use a tool that was specifically created for that purpose. There are project management tools that already exist and will make your life so much easier. I have yet to find a project management tool that fits any of my clients 100%, so the best I can suggest is to do your own research and find one that you resonate with the most.

Some of these tools are free to use, others only offer free trials. See which one suits you best, depending on your preferences on usability, design, and functionality and choose one.

When setting up the project plan, we want to take everything we have already created and bring it into one big picture and add our action steps.

For our example, we have already set our goal, prioritized it as the #1 task to work on, broke it down into 3-month milestones, further down into a 1-month roadmap resulting in monthly targets and weekly focus topics. We also calculated the time needed to fulfill these steps including buffer times. We are ready to go.

For most of these tools there will be an initial set up necessary that will help you to create a realistic plan. Check the settings of your tool and see what conditions you are able to set up for your project plan. One popular rule for example is: "Do not count Saturday and Sunday as working days." Since our focus fund says we have 3.5 days per week to dedicate to work, we will block out the other 3.5 days as off days. You can choose whichever days you like best.

To begin, choose one of the following options that best reflects what you want your project plan to look like. The following three project planning methods are the most common and the easiest to work with:

GANTT CHART

Henry Gantt designed the first version of this chart somewhere around 1910. The Gantt Chart looks like a spreadsheet with a timeline on the top row and the tasks that need to be fulfilled in the first column. Colored bars fill the slots of time that each task will take. This creates a visual project plan, including tasks that overlap. In modern Gantt Charts it is also possible to include responsibilities, dependency relationships between tasks, and the current status of the project plan. For analytical minds, the Gantt Chart is a great way to immediately see the status of the project and get valuable data from it.

GANTT CHART

Task Name	Jan	Feb	Mar	Apr	May	Jun
Planning		███				
Research			███			
Design				███		
Implementation					███	
Follow up						███

 www.moniquelindner.com    @themoniquelindner

KANBAN BOARD

Imagine a kanban board as a digital version of the sticky notes on a poster that you can drag and drop as you please. Instead of sticky notes, we create cards that can be attached to different lists on our board. Each card is filled with information about one specific task, the responsible person, a deadline, a description of the task, a possible dependency relationship, and files as an attachment if needed. The lists show the progress of the project, and are often labeled with generic names such as "To Do", "In Progress", "For Review", "Done," and others. For visual learners, it can be easier to grasp a project plan in the form of a kanban board, which offers a big-picture overview to see which tasks are being worked on, which ones need reviewing, and which are left.

CALENDAR VIEW

The calendar view offers a rather granular view of the tasks. It shows the daily, weekly, and monthly breakdown of tasks and the dates for when they are assigned. This view is a great add-on for the Gantt Chart or kanban board in order to go more into detail. As a standalone project plan, it makes sense when planning out the 1-month roadmap, particularly when there are specific days that need to be blocked for things like holidays and appointments and hence need a workaround in planning.

CALENDAR

Sunday	Monday	Tuesday	Wednesday	Thursday	Friday	Saturday
		1	2 Team breakfast	3	4	5
6	7	8	9	10 Lunch with Anna	11	12
13	14 Preparing presentation	15	16 Presentation	17	18 Finance report	19
20	21	22	23	24 Meeting with Monique	25	26
27	28	29 Marketing planning	30 Product review	31		

 www.moniquelindner.com   @themoniquelindner

Most of the project planning tools out there offer all three of these methods. The difference lies in the visual presentation and how you work with tasks and dependencies between them.

Depending on which visual plan you are using, you can now input all details to set up the project plan, the timeline, and milestones for this project. Be aware of any projects that need to be completed before others can start, be mindful of deadlines, and don't forget buffer times!

Since we are only planning a single month this process is fairly simple. If you want to follow along while I work this out in real time, visit www.thetimemethod.com/bookexperience to watch the pre-recorded planning video.

SECTION 5| Scheduling

Now that we've got all the goodies planned out, we can get to scheduling them. Pheeew. Can you feel the excitement? I know what you're thinking. "What do you mean 'excitement?' This took me freaking *days* to do and now she's trying to tell me this can be part of my life? Hell nah!"

I promise you, this is only taking so long right now because 1) I am talking quite a bit and it takes a little while to walk you through everything, and 2) I want you to really get this right and practice it until it becomes natural. The time management stuff is tedious for many people because they don't know how they can integrate it into their daily lives, but I promise it gets better, and the best is yet to come.

Looking at all of your now-prioritized tasks and goals, you can probably see light at the end of the tunnel. This is especially true after you cut out the unnecessary and prioritize the important over the urgent. To tighten up your task list, we now want to schedule everything out. That is the ultimate step to finally get moving in the right direction: straight towards your goals, instead of wasting time along the way.

Stephen Covey said, "The key is not to prioritize what's on your schedule, but to schedule your priorities." That is exactly what we will do in the coming section. Scheduling our priorities will look different for each of us, not only in regards to the particular priorities we appoint but also in terms of the time of day we will work on them.

Some of us like to work early in the morning while others would rather stay up late and get their work done then. Differences also depend on lifestyle, routines, and other preferences. The science behind it has a lot to do with our chronotype, which I explained in the Foundations chapter at the beginning of the book. Our chronotype massively influences which times are more productive for us and which times we feel rather low in energy and should therefore use for chores, low-level priority tasks, or appointments that don't need our full attention such as going to the dentist or to the hair stylist.

For best scheduling results, we will first need to find your most productive times. When I say most productive times I actually mean the best time to work on your most important tasks (MIT). If we look at this from a scientific standpoint, it is usually around 2 to 4 hours after you first wake up, sometimes right after that. The MIT should be the first task to get done before you do anything else work-wise, even before emails and messages or any other tasks.

We only have a certain amount of "brain mass" we can work with every day, just like a phone battery. Our brain "battery" gets recharged in our sleep while it is pruned of unnecessary information, giving us fresh brain mass to work with in the morning. From then on, every decision we make, every step we take, every task we get done, every thought we think drains this brain mass a little more, just like our phone battery is drained as we use more apps and keep our screen on longer.

No study has yet given a fixed number, but scientists suggest that the average total length of time a person can do focused work (not interrupted, non-focused, or social-media-scrolling busywork, but actual, focused, important-tasks work) is around 4 hours or less. That may freak you out a little bit and make you wonder, "How in the entrepreneurial world am I gonna get A L L O F T H E T A S K S done in just 4 hours?" Yep. It's possible, and by the end of this book you'll know how.

Working with your chrono-energy types here will make a huge difference. For almost all of the chrono-energy types, I recommend starting with the most important tasks each and every day. Mostly because when your brain mass is fresh, decisions can be made with a clear head, solutions are found more quickly and efficiently, and fewer mistakes are made.

What comes after that depends on your chrono-energy type and how your work day looks. If your energy is low but still okay to work, then category 3 work, repetitive tasks, admin work, and appointments and calls are good for these time slots. If your energy is super low, then you need to recharge with food, a nap, a walk, or some exercise, depending again on your chrono-energy type. It often takes a little bit to get back into work right after these time slots. If that's the case, it's also a good time for category 3 work.

When your energy is no longer at its highest, but still charged (or re-charged) enough, this is the time for all category 2 tasks, or calls and appointments that require a lot of listening and thinking from your end.

Now that we've got that figured out, let's go through scheduling together. This is going to be easy-peasy-pineapple-squeezy!

Just as we only want to plan for three months at a time, we only want to look one week ahead when scheduling. Things can change quickly, and we want to be able to adapt and be flexible. I recommend sitting down on a Sunday evening to schedule out the following week. This should not take longer than 30 minutes once you have incorporated a planning practice that works well for you.

Start with a *weekly review* of what went well and what can be improved from the week before. I do this by answering these 5 questions:

1| List all wins you experienced, no matter how little or big!

2| What are the lessons you learned?

3| How can you implement what you learned into your daily operation?

4| Are there any tasks that need a change in prioritization?

5| What do you want to do differently or keep doing next week to keep your energy high, feel joy while working, and feel accomplished by the end of the week?

The most essential step that simply can not be skipped is prioritization. The sooner you can tell the difference between tasks that totally need to get done and those that are just a nice add-on, the sooner you can make peace with the idea that some tasks simply may not get done for whatever reason. Once you've made that peace, you will have a fuller battery and also be able to get all tasks done in a better state of flow. Surrender to the idea of not finishing your to-do list each day and be happy and satisfied with knocking off the top 3 tasks. You'll see how much more energy you have left to do the rest, too… should you choose to do them.

As a little refresher from the last section, we spoke about the following prioritization methods:

- The Eisenhower Box: Do, Decide, Delegate and Delete

- The Traffic Light: Red, Yellow, Green

- 2 Strikes Rule: Yes & Yes, Yes for Money/No for Time, Yes for Time/No for Money, No & No

- The SSP: Most Important Tasks (MIT), Secondary Tasks (ST), Additional Tasks (AT)

Now that we know how our tasks are prioritized and categorized, we can start scheduling the weekly focus topics we created during our 1-Month Roadmap, including the task list which we have now prioritized. Whichever prioritization method you choose to use doesn't matter — it just matters that you use one!

The goal here is to keep this stupid simple, since this will be done weekly. The more you do it, the better you will get at it. It now takes me 10 or 15 minutes each Sunday to schedule out my week after writing out my tasks and prioritizing them, which itself takes no longer than 15 or 20 minutes. The weekly review is another wonderful way for me to look at my progress for the last week and get excited for the next week, so that Monday morning I wake up full of energy and ready to go.

Before we get into scheduling our week, I'd like to give you some guidelines that will be important no matter the tasks on your list.

1| PLAN YOUR TIME OFF FIRST

In Section 2 we spoke about off days and the importance of prioritizing them in our schedule. Now is the time to implement what we learned. **Start your weekly schedule by planning your time off**. If you chose to create a focus fund, you already know exactly how many days to block. In our example, we have 3.5 off days per week. These do not necessarily need to be consecutive days off. Some people choose to spread their off days out throughout the week. Others split them across days and work half-days every day. Schedule all celebrations, holidays, and other special occasions as extra time off as well.

The more realistic our schedule looks timewise, the more realistic our expectations can be in regards to what we can achieve and how many tasks we can add to the schedule.

2| PLAN NON-NEGOTIABLES SECOND

Once you have your time off scheduled, we **move on to non-negotiable appointments, health & wellness, and chores** such as visits to the doctor, wellness treatments, appointments with your kids and/or partner, household chores, and others that are non-negotiable. For best results when working through your tasks list, I recommend scheduling your non-negotiables during the times that you are lower on energy, outside of your most productive times. Many of our non-negotiables are necessary treatments for self-care which will fill up our energy levels, or else things like doctors visits that don't need your full energy.

We schedule time off and non-negotiable appointments separately from our priority list because high achievers tend not to not give them any priority at all. Let me take a guess: the tasks on your priority list are nearly all business-related. Of course. That is what we are taught. In order to create time for *you* and the really incredibly important things outside of business, we schedule them first and do not include them in our priority system. I also strongly believe that when we take care of ourselves first, it allows us to take care of everything else with our fullest energy.

Once you've got your schedule filled with off time and non-negotiable appointments, you now have a realistic picture of how many hours you are free to spend on work.

Scheduling works best when you follow this simple process: The 1-2-2 Rule. This rule will give you a simple structure for *what* type of tasks to schedule in your day. By keeping your chrono-energy type in mind, you can then decide *when* you will work on these tasks throughout the day so that you can manage your energy most efficiently.

→ THE 1-2-2 RULE

This rule is seriously simple, yet many people struggle to implement it because it looks like we are not adding enough tasks to our day. Our mind wants us to add more and more and more.

In short, we are going to schedule 5 tasks per day.

One Most Important Task (from Category 1)

Two Secondary Tasks (from Category 2) and

Two Additional Tasks (from Category 3)

That's it.

The focus here is to get the Most Important Task (MIT) done. Best case scenario we do it first thing in the morning, every day. There are a few reasons for this. The people who prefer to add the MIT in the morning want to "eat the frog" first, so to speak. Many studies have shown a variety of good reasons for doing the hardest task first. For one, our brains are at their freshest in the morning. After waking up in the morning from its nightly pruning and detox, our brains are primed for decision making, thinking, processing, emotions, and so on. It's working at 100% capacity.

Working on the hardest task in the morning makes sense neuroscientifically. On the psychological side, accomplishing the MIT first also drives in a big win, creating momentum for the day. This activates our neurotransmitters to produce dopamine, which makes us feel rewarded, leaving us with a feeling of happiness and pride.

Last but not least, this strategy also helps people who tend to procrastinate on big, difficult tasks. If you set a daily challenge for yourself that you can't do anything else until you finish your MIT, you better believe you'll find a way to do it. Making it a game is even better, especially if you are a super-procrastinator. Join accountability groups and bet against yourself to actually put some money behind your challenge.

When you schedule your week, put the MITs down as the first task every morning. These times should be blocked out for only that task. Make sure that you have no non-negotiables in there unless it is inevitable.

After scheduling your MITs, we will take care of the Secondary Tasks (STs). Each day we have two slots where STs are scheduled. Based on your chrono-energy type you can decide where these best fit into your daily routine. This can widely vary from person to person. Know that you want your energy level to be at least 60% or more for working on your Secondary Tasks, as they are often tasks that do need our presence and brain mass more than Additional Tasks (ATs) and we want to make sure that we have the energy to be attentive for them.

If you are able to focus for a while, based on your productivity type, you may schedule the two slots in one go. Make sure to calculate a break of at least 30 minutes between the two slots for you to move, stretch, drink water, and get away from the screen for a while. If your productivity type is on the shorter end of focusing, schedule the task out over several smaller slots.

Lastly, when we schedule our Additional Tasks, we are looking at a few different possibilities. Are we filling in gaps during our schedule with these tasks? Do we batch them all into one day by the end of the week? Are these tasks we can do by the end of our working day? Whatever feels best to you is the way to go here. The goal is to fill 2 slots per day. Most of the ATs will not take as much brain space and energy as our MITs or STs, so it is absolutely okay to do them when your energy is on the lower end of the scale.

Having said all of that, we can finally take our prioritized task list that we created based on our weekly focus topic for the upcoming week and start scheduling our tasks out. YAY!

# CHAPTER REVIEW

This was a hell of a chapter. In our review, we will go over the steps in this chapter from a birds-eye view, adding some action steps for you to implement right now.

1| GOAL SETTING

Look at the different versions of goals described in this section.

Which of them do you resonate with the most?

1. Start with the goal that is furthest away in time and follow the exercise that you feel most comfortable with

2. You can do one or all of the exercises in the chapter. Keep in mind that we are looking for quality over quantity

3. Set at least one S.M.A.R.T. goal for yourself for 12 months from now

2| OFF DAYS

Take some time to look at the next 6-12 months ahead. Have you planned any time off yet?

1. If yes, is it enough and is it on a regular basis?

2. If no, can you add some time off to your regular schedule right now?

When can you commit to planning your year based on the time off you'd love to have in your life?

3. Put a reminder in your calendar and start then

4. Create your focus fund

3| PRIORITIZING

Take your task list for the upcoming week or create a task list with all recurring tasks that are usually on your list.

1. Choose one of the methods of prioritization in Section 3

2. Practice it with your current task list or the one you have just created

4| PLANNING

Go back to Section 4 with your newly set S.M.A.R.T. goal in hand.

1. Walk through the process step by step

2. Keep going

5| SCHEDULING

You now should have two things: a project plan that shows you what your goal looks like in achievable action steps and the time it will take to achieve them, and a list of tasks that you will work on to achieve your weekly focus topic over the upcoming week.

1. If you are not sure how we got here, go back through the previous section

2. Take your prioritized task list and schedule your upcoming week

WOAH. What an achievement to not only make it through this chapter, but also implement all action steps. This alone needs celebrating! Hot damn, you are my kinda person!

Impactful Leadership

Leadership is a big gift and an even bigger responsibility. Very few people are naturally gifted leaders, and the ones who are often live trauma-ridden lives before unwrapping their gift for the world.

I have been in a position of leadership many times in my life. Sometimes I naturally stepped into the role; other times I was asked or voted to lead a group of people or a team.

I remember quite a few of these instances happening when I was as young as 5 years old. I guess it was partly because I was always very happy to make decisions. I was also always pretty successful at inspiring groups to follow my lead. But I believe that there's a more important reason that I was so frequently chosen as a leader: I took responsibility, and I didn't fold when things got ugly. I stood my ground, and I stood it firm.

There were times when people in my group or team would make mistakes, but because it was my responsibility to make sure people got things right, I would take the consequences. Don't get me wrong, even as a child I wouldn't let other kids get away with messing things up out of carelessness or irresponsibility. But I'm sure it was much nicer for them to deal with me than with the adults. Much later on, in my corporate career, this paid off big time.

At the tender age of 22 I was hired as the team and process manager for the IT 2nd level support of Siemens Enterprise Networks (SEN). The company was in the middle of a shift from Siemens to SEN and was struggling to remotely migrate 25,000 people to new operating systems, software, and server setups. The tech support I was hired to manage simply couldn't keep up with tens of thousands of support tickets and calls made daily about all of the issues that occurred during the migration. I was hired to fix the mess, or at least pretend to do so. No one actually believed that I would be instrumental to the project since I was new to IT.

I may have been new to IT, but I wasn't new to leadership. My intuition told me that this team didn't have an issue with tech knowledge or performance. It was the processes and the team structure itself that were a mess, plus people were simply overworked. But when you come into a world that is (according to society's rules and expectations) not supposed to be yours, and you bring ideas that are outside of the box, you better believe that every single cell of basically every single person is up against you. That opposition has nothing to do with you as a person, and that is probably the most important lesson that every leader must learn.

After all these years in leadership positions, team management, and traveling, these are my top 3 lessons:

Lesson 1: Take nothing personally, even when people make you feel like their feelings and actions are personal. Everything is a reflection of perception.

Lesson 2: Trust your intuition. Trust yourself. Trust in your own actions.

Lesson 3: Listen to understand. Listen to learn. Listen to support.

I could probably write a whole book on lessons learned from 17 + years of leadership. And maybe I will. It sounds like something I would read, too. But back to this book.

I am sure you've already come to understand that leadership is not an easy undertaking. I have seen leaders who tried hard but didn't implement their strategies very well, I have seen others who did outright miserable jobs and, unfortunately, I have seen just a few that I look up to and celebrate as true leaders.

In 2020, it's not just enough to simply manage a team or be good at project or time management. That is not leadership. Leadership is so much more, and in this chapter I want to show you what this means.

I am writing this book in 2020. Yep, that's right. I mean *that* 2020 … with a pandemic taking over the planet...resulting in the crash of the economy...and the lockdown of basically the whole world...in the middle of a civil rights movement raising awareness about racial injustice. Yep, *that* 2020.

I am listing these global crises to show you why it is not enough to just manage time or manage projects or even manage people. In order to be able to get through crises like this and come out stronger on a personal, business and/or collective level, we need more people stepping into leadership. This does not mean that it is everyone's job to be a leader and it also does not mean that everyone should take over a civil rights movement. There is a place and a role for everyone and throughout the next chapter it will become clear which is yours to take on.

This year punched us in the collective face over and over again. And it finally calls us to step up and lead. Before I explain what I mean by that, let me explain what leadership is not:

THE BOSS

Leadership is not just bossing people around, ordering people to do things that are actually your job out of convenience or just because you can. Being an asshole also has nothing to do with being a leader, nor is it helpful in 95% of situations. Being "bossy" at all times is simply a cover-up for your own insecurities (uh oh, now we are getting straight to the harsh truth). In all of my experiences with bossy people, and I promise there have been *a lot* of them, there was not a single person that wasn't using this type of behavior as a cover-up for their feelings of inadequacy.

Being the boss was trendy before women were allowed to vote. As you may have noticed, things have changed, and so should you.

THE MANAGER

The "manager" style of leadership is a step in the right direction, but with one big issue: He is a control freak. Not only does he control every bit of his own life, but he also loves micromanaging his team and all of their moves. What they do, when they do it, how they are doing it...and if it's not the way he wants them to do it, they'll have to re-do it, even if the results turn out exactly the way he wanted.

Sounds exhausting? It is. And it's not only exhausting for the team members on the receiving end, it's also exhausting for the manager himself. Or in my case, herself. I was this kind of person. Control can kill a lot of things, such as efficiency, team spirit, and joy. The manager is not the only person on a team who tends to abuse control, but they are usually one of the main characters.

Another reason we don't want to just "manage" people is because this style is missing a whole aspect of leadership. Giving up control is an opportunity that leads to more creativity, a more independent team, and better solutions.

THE PEOPLE-PLEASER.

The last of the 3 "bad leader archetypes" that we do not want to embody is the people-pleaser. The people-pleaser is basically the opposite of the boss, but more annoying, and no less frustrating. Full disclosure: I am a recovering people-pleaser and, wow, what a process that's been. My journey into and through leadership opened my eyes and transformed me into a non-people-pleaser. I now love myself and stand firm in who I am. I am more than grateful to have had to learn that.

People-pleasing has absolutely nothing to do with leadership. Saying yes to everything will not make you a leader, and it won't even make everyone like you. Quite the opposite is true, actually. If you can't say no, you end up putting yourself and people on your team into precarious and unprofessional situations. This can happen when you take on way too many clients or agree to projects that can't actually be properly fulfilled, thereby accumulating an impossible, unhealthy, or physically dangerous workload for your team. Being afraid to say no also becomes awkward for you personally, like when you continue to promise certain deadlines or outcomes for your clients while simultaneously allowing your team to delay work or take vacations.

Now that we understand how *not* to be a leader, let's finally talk about how to be a leader, as well as some of the personal risks.

SECTION 1| What Does Modern Leadership Look Like & Why Do We Need It?

Modern leadership sounds so … 2020. In this day and age, it is not just about what kind of leader you are and how you face the world, but also about what you do with the influence you have.

Will you use your influence for social impact? Are you going to make yourself rich, or will you spread the wealth across communities? Will you share opportunities with people who otherwise wouldn't have a chance, people who would need to work much harder and longer than you would?

The Good Finance project defines social impact as the *"effect on people and communities that happens as a result of an action or inaction, an activity, project, programme or policy."*

To me, social impact means creating opportunities for underserved people and communities with and through your business. This could be through financial support, education, and job opportunities, or through volunteering your time, skills, knowledge, resources, or equipment to projects supporting a specific cause that is aligned with your core values.

But why am I asking the modern leader to take responsibility for social impact? Why don't we let the peace-loving, lifetime-activist, vegan hippies (I am stereotyping, please stay with me for a moment) take care of social impact? Because we need both. This is 2020, the year everyone won the bullshit bingo.

We need more than a handful of people worrying about the good of this planet and the people who live here.

We need the hippie activists. We need the ranting vegans. We need the "don't you dare!" environmentalists. And we also need the New Age entrepreneurs (you!) to step up into social impact leadership. We also need a whole new generation of politicians, but let's stick to the book.

Social impact leaders are often entrepreneurs or business owners for one very specific reason. They have a skill that's very much needed, whether we like it or not: making money. But we don't need to make money to just throw it around aimlessly. We need to make money, and then we need to be able to assess where money needs to be invested, and where resources need to be created, people need to be hired, training needs to be organized, and so on. Right now, humanity's most powerful vehicle to equity is money, and as entrepreneurs, we know how to make it in creative ways. I use the word vehicle on purpose because money is NOT the most powerful asset. Time is.

Another reason impactful leadership is important is because of the lifestyles so many of us are able to live in the modern era. Our access to high-quality, comfortable lives have pushed our brains out of survival mode and into a new phenomenon I have noticed with entrepreneurs all over the world. As soon as we reach a point where we are no longer struggling for money, we crave a purpose, a reason for living and working. Our "why."

It can take a long time to understand that your "why," your purpose, is always bigger than yourself. It's what makes every fight worth fighting. Many of us have families, which become the reason why many of us do what we do, and yet we still yearn for a larger purpose. That's when social impact comes into the game.

Social impact is a win-win for all parties involved when set up correctly. It helps the people and communities who are receiving aid, and it gives the person who is organizing or contributing this help a bigger purpose, which will have just as valuable an impact on their life, too.

Though social impact leaders do often come from business or entrepreneurship, it is so important that our modern leaders come from every walk of life. We need leaders from all different nationalities, religions, tribes, backgrounds, races, abilities and needs, genders, and love preferences. From every community. Representation matters. Like a herd of wolves, we are only as strong as the "weakest" in our group. We need leaders who come from the groups that society calls "weak" because they know best how we can empower them.

So now we know *why* we need modern leadership, and what it *shouldn't* look like... but what *does* modern leadership look like?

Over the past 20 years working for, with, and beside other people I have found the following list most true when answering the question, "What makes a good leader."

1| Kindness. If you are an unkind person, please don't even think about becoming a leader. We already have enough assholes in leadership positions, and the world needs more kindness. But don't mistake kindness for weakness. Kindness has nothing to do with being nice, or with a lack of boundaries or firmness. To be kind is to see the humanity in the person sitting across from you and treating them the way you would want to be treated, no matter how they may have treated you or what they have done wrong.

Being kind is not the same as being "nice" to someone who treated you badly. You can—and should—hold them accountable, set boundaries, talk about rules, walk them through consequences, and have difficult conversations all in a very kind way. You can also let emotions get the best of you and treat them like an inferior being who deserves nothing but harsh unkindness. A leader, though, doesn't do that. A good modern leader understands the power of kindness.

2| Compassion. If we do not have compassion as a leader we won't be trusted by the people that we lead. Compassion is different from sympathy and empathy. It's the ability to feel for another person and their experiences without taking on their feelings for yourself. As a leader, and especially a leader with social impact, it is incredibly important to be able to see, understand, and listen to other people and let them know they are safe with you.

Empathy allows us to understand and share the emotions of another person, which means that we can put ourselves in their shoes and truly feel what they feel. This can be helpful for personal relationships and intimate work, but it's dangerous in leadership. It can drown you in a sea of emotions and creates a risk of burnout by draining your energy faster than a power surge kills a phone battery. If you are an empath, it's important to set strong boundaries and maintain a de-stress regimen, a supportive network, and a good mental health routine.

Sympathy, on the other hand, is a feeling of pity or sorrow for someone else. It's meant to be a kind gesture, but it is unfortunately often misplaced, especially when you don't truly understand the other person or their situation. That's when we give unsolicited advice that is well-meant but not well received for many different reasons.

Good leaders need to be able to feel compassion without feeling pity. And contrary to the empath, compassionate leaders need to avoid taking on anyone else's feelings and emotions as their own. This is how we lead well while keeping our mental health in order and our energy safe and protected at all times.

3| Boundaries. The ability to set strong boundaries, keep them in place, and communicate them kindly but firmly is one of the most important and hard-won qualities of a good leader. I can not count the number of times I've had to stand up for myself and explain, defend, explain again, and again, and listen to every reason why my boundaries are unacceptable, unnecessary, ridiculous, or whatever the other person decided that day… it's exhausting, to say the least. And not only is it a clear form of disrespecting boundaries, it can also become a form of manipulation, gaslighting, and toxic behavior. In Chapter 7 I will share more about what this looks like and why it makes setting boundaries so much harder.

Boundaries are not taught in school, and they are often not taught by our families, either. Quite the opposite. That meant that we grew up at the mercy of expectations without being able to protect ourselves from their hypocrisy. As a girl (and now, as a woman), I was told to always say yes (and amen) to everything, not "make a scene", to not "be a bitch", to not be "bossy", to not be too loud, too deciding, too independent, too hyperactive, cry too much, not to wear too much makeup, or not enough, wear "revealing" clothes, or "manly" clothes … and with all of these expectations there was NO WAY to get it right. If only I was taught to set boundaries, I would have been able to see those things for what they were: a set of hypocritical societal expectations.

Society, and by that I mean our families, friends, teachers and other authority figures, didn't stop at making "rules" for women. There is a whole set for men, too. And as you can see, you can NEVER fulfill them, so it doesn't make any sense to try. Quite frankly, I stopped trying a while ago. So what to do instead? Set your own rules and boundaries, but do not limit yourself with them, either. As a leader, it is critical to have a clear understanding of expectations, standards, and boundaries, which is why we will talk about all three in depth in Chapter 7.

4| Growth Mindset. As a leader it is necessary to be willing to be wrong and open to hearing that you are. A growth mindset helps to do so, because it allows you to understand other people's perspectives and to see that your lens comes from your own experiences, lessons, and upbringing, but that these circumstances don't apply to everyone. A growth mindset will help you keep an open mind and lead discussions without pushing your own opinion onto others.

The central feature of a growth mindset is the understanding that skills can be learned, knowledge can be gained, and that everyone can be successful and change their circumstances through effort. This is specifically useful in the hiring process, as it will guide you towards focusing on core values rather than individual skills, enabling you to build strong and loyal teams.

5| Strong opinions. Let's make one thing clear first: Great leaders do not have to be controversial, nor are controversial people good leaders. That's such a weird misconception that probably comes with the social media influencer wave, where people can become "famous" by saying random controversial things just for the sake of stirring the pot. That is not leadership. That is poor engagement tactics and desperation.

Having a strong opinion is necessary. Knowing how to communicate it is even more important. As a leader we must be able to take a stance, make a point, and stand up for our beliefs. That is how we can create a movement. But we are not here to blame, shame, or harm other people with our opinions. We are not here to hurt others intentionally or put others down in order to feel better about ourselves. It's quite the opposite. We are here to lift others up by sharing our experiences, our opinions, and our beliefs, and by highlighting the voices of those who don't have the strength, courage, confidence, power, or platform to do so.

6| Be a lifelong student. This should be a simple one, yet I see so many people in leadership positions who are not willing to be a student. They think they have reached a point where they have nothing more to learn, or they believe that they are superior and others have nothing to teach them. Or maybe, and this goes back to the growth mindset, they are preventing themselves from being able to learn more. Whatever the reason, it will keep them from being a great leader.

Leaders learn on a daily basis, through every interaction. In every experience, there is always a lesson, a fact, or a new perspective to learn. Being a student has nothing to do with being in school. There are so many different ways to study that have nothing to do with academic knowledge. Traveling to or living in different countries, listening to podcasts, talking to or interviewing people with different perspectives and experiences, trying out new experiences, foods, and lifestyles yourself are all ways to study. So is unplugging from the social and digital worlds completely to spend an extended time outdoors connecting deeper with yourself and the natural world.

There are infinite ways to learn and study. The goal is not to do all of these things, but to do the ones that resonate with you, and do them intentionally. And never stop learning.

7| Be a teacher. Great leaders should always be learning, and they should always share what they have learned. When you take on a leadership role, people will want to learn from you. They will ask questions and are looking for answers.

I urge you to be very diligent with the knowledge that you share. We have a word in German for spreading superficial knowledge, or talking about things we've heard of but actually know nothing about (looking at you, keyboard warriors on social media!). We call it *halbwissen*, which translates literally to "half-knowledge." In a world of Google, Youtube, and Instagram, we think we have everything at our fingertips, but the due diligence to actually do research often goes out the window. Researching, learning about, and understanding a topic to form your own opinion is completely different than doing a Google search.

As a leader, it is critical to only share knowledge that is based in study, hence why being a lifelong student is so important. Being able to share that knowledge in a way that people from many different walks of life can understand and digest it is what makes a good teacher. Both of these skills together are two important parts of what it takes to be a good leader. Then again, each of us is not for everyone, so there will always be people who won't understand what you share and that's okay.

8| Be a guide. For those that do understand your teachings and want to learn more, you will be a guide. You will also be a guide for people who come from a similar background to your own and who wish to follow your lead, your example, or your successes. Others will recognize and see things in you that you may not see for yourself, and look to you for guidance anyway.

I love to use the analogy of the tour guides I had the pleasure to be guided by on different travel experiences. One in particular that comes to my mind is the guide that took me on a 5-day tour into the deepest jungle of the Bolivian Amazon. We were a group of five (two couples and myself) and he asked for our expectations and hopes for the tour. Mine were to swim with pink freshwater dolphins and to find a wild anaconda. Yeah, I'm that kind of person. He laughed and told me that it was extremely rare to find a wild anaconda, but he knew where they usually stick around, and he would do his best but couldn't promise anything. Great expectation setting! But what made this guide so truly great was that not only did he ask for and set our expectations, but he answered all questions along the way, taught us about the animals and their behavior, helped people out along the way, and told some jokes to keep people entertained. And he did find an anaconda for us!

See, he could have been a people-pleaser, promising us things that he wasn't sure he'd be able to fulfill, but he was not. He also made sure to keep people in a good mood. For example, one of the couples was moody and full of complaints. Our guide realized that this could be a dealbreaker for the whole group, so he always made sure to keep everyone in good spirits. A good guide can lead a group, set expectations well, and keep them in good spirits until a goal is achieved. A great guide can also sense when the mood swings, when an issue may arise, and when expectations have to be reset, and then react accordingly.

9| Intention. Your intention is just as powerful and as important as your purpose and will set you up for success or for failure. Take stock of your soul and ask yourself what your intention is behind being a leader. Why do you really want to take this on and become the kind of person that is able to do any of this? What is it that excites you about being an impactful leader in today's world?

To answer that question, we need to examine the definition of intention. In this case we are talking about the idea, the reasoning, or the concept driving your actions. Your purpose, on the other hand, is a greater goal bigger than yourself that you would like to achieve. This is your driving force for being a leader. In other words, your intentions are the "how" behind showing up as a leader and your purpose is the "why" you became a leader in the first place.

As a leader it is very important to have intentions and a purpose that are supportive of the collective, not just yourself. Which brings me straight to the next point.

10| Fighting for the greater good rather than credit/status. You might think, "well duh, doesn't a leader help other people?" They do. But many leaders do so to polish up their social status, to receive credit and brag with it, to get the validation they never received, and overall, just to look good. If you are only acting as a leader to collect a medal for your work, you may as well stop right here. This is not helping the greater good. Your ego and need for validation will stand in the way of actually helping the collective in ways they truly need rather than the ways that would make you look good.

As humans we all carry cognitive biases within us. Some of these biases can change the way that we help others. Sometimes, we help others the way we think is best, rather than the way they actually need. This is called a "savior complex," especially when the person helping is also showing off their "help" for social status. I have seen this way too often in the volunteer world. It is difficult for people who are in need to stand up and say no to this behavior, because while they do need aid, they don't want to be exploited for the savior's need of validation.

Set your intentions straight and fight for the right reasons, not just for the status and the credit that might come with the work you do. I promise, at least 95% of the good things I have done in this world are unknown to anyone. And this includes some very big things, too. But I have been taught since childhood to "do good, and don't talk about it," or else it's not a good deed. I don't fully agree with this, because I believe that storytelling is a powerful tool to raise awareness and to share the needs of others. Just make sure that the spotlight is on the story being shared, and not on us.

11 | Willingness to heal. You can't heal if you don't acknowledge you have been hurt. Let that sink in. Now, read it again, slowly. You can't heal if you don't acknowledge you have been hurt.

I believe one of our biggest strengths as leaders is our own healing, and the permission we give others, through our own processing, to heal, too. The beautiful but painful process opens eyes, ears, and hearts, and that is why we need to be willing to heal what has hurt us. Not all at once. Not all of it today. But step by step, wound by wound, person by person, bit by bit, until we are whole.

That doesn't mean we can't lead until we are whole, but we can't lead until we have at least started the process. If you now feel the resistance creeping in, whispering, "I don't have anything to heal, I wasn't hurt, there is no trauma"… then this part is 100% for you. Maybe you haven't seen it. Maybe you are looking away. Maybe you are missing something. Or maybe you have already been through your healing journey, in which case there should be no resistance, only pure joy and inner knowing that these words are true. If you did feel resistance, pay attention to where it came up for you, what it told you, what it tried to point out for you. Then follow it.

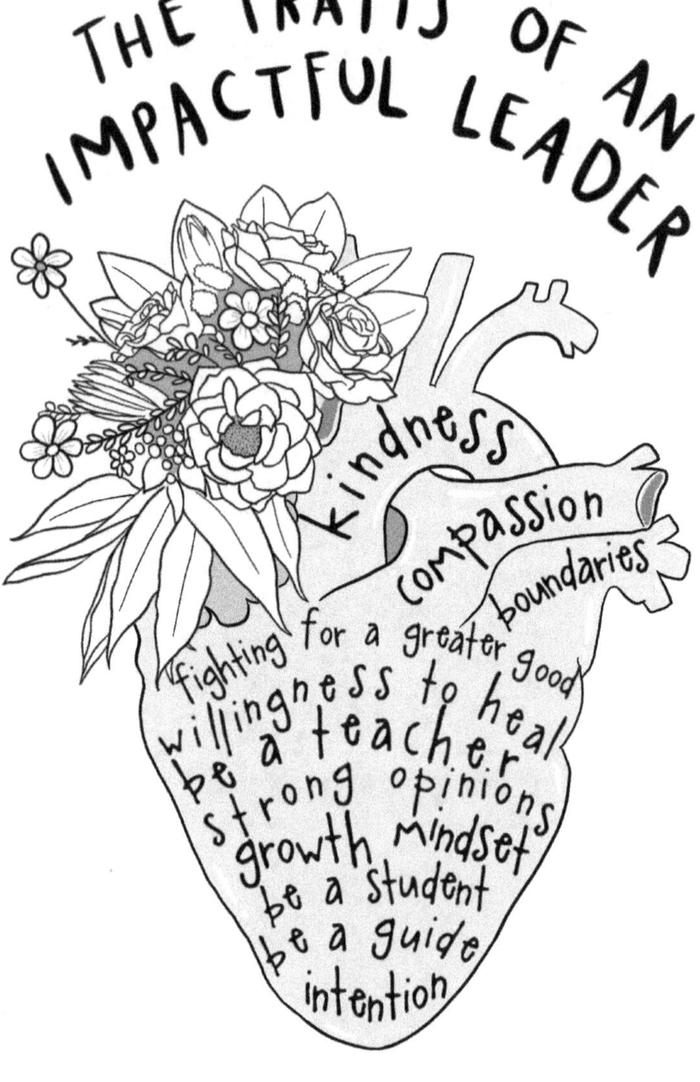

THE TRAITS OF AN IMPACTFUL LEADER

Now that I've listed the 11 qualities of good leaders, I want to share one more thing: Please don't be a leader.

Don't get me wrong. I really do want you to step up to be an impactful leader. What I am saying is this: we don't need leaders that do it for the credit, the money, the status, and the spotlight. We also absolutely don't need those online influencers turned wannabe-leaders. And for the record, people with these behaviors ain't leaders. Even though they may have good intentions.

What we do need are impactful leaders, yet not everyone should be, can be, or will be a good leader. And that is 100% okay. If you are one of the many people who doesn't even want to be a leader, then please know that we also need amazing supporters. We need people to cheer leaders on, support them, hold them accountable, push them, and help implement the necessary action steps. If this is you, then I celebrate you and I want you to own this and be proud.

If you are feeling called to be a leader, please take an honest assessment of the steps above. Decide truthfully whether or not you have integrated all of the traits of good leadership, even if some of them are not yet fully developed. If you see yourself in one of the shortcomings I called out but still believe that you are a leader and that you should be on the front line, please take a step back and reconsider your decision. Look at the world and what is really needed.

Leadership has nothing to do with your individual needs and everything to do with the collective good. If you can not see this, whether ego is in your way or you feel resistance coming up, then this is your call to look again.

SECTION 2| Burnout Is Real — And How To Prevent It

I was 19 when I had my first burnout, and it killed me. I didn't realize what I had experienced was a burnout until I had a second one, and I was afraid I'd ended up with another cardiac arrest. Instead of a clinical death, everything just got a little more painful the second round, a series of signals from life that I should make sure this was the last burnout I ever went through.

One of those signals was an excruciating spine injury. Four discs along my spine prolapsed and herniated. One of them cut off my spinal cord, which resulted in extremely painful paralysis of my right leg.

What does this have to do with burn out? Our body, mind, and spirit all work together as a unit. If one is out of whack, the other two are weakened and become easier to hurt. Burnout happens when your mind is pushed to the limit and your body is exhausted. It is a state of complete depletion. There is no back or forth and you end up with tunnel vision where all you can see is misery with no way to turn out of it. You feel like you have to just push forward to get out of it so you do, you push and push and push, but all you do is sink deeper into the problem.

You can compare this to an inexperienced swimmer who gets caught up in a rip current in the open ocean. Rip currents are dangerous because once a person gets in and doesn't know how to get out, they usually try to swim against the current. The current is the strongest and fastest on the surface of the water, and it will drag the struggling person straight out into the open ocean. Most of the time people who drown in rip currents do so because of a combination of fear or panic and exhaustion.

Fear and exhaustion! That's exactly why people burn out, too. You get caught in the rip current of work and life, and oftentimes it feels like you are drowning. Drowning in work, drowning in expectations, drowning in shame and guilt, or drowning in pain.

In my own experience, and having had quite a few friends who have unfortunately experienced their own burnouts, it can take years to recover from burnout if you don't catch it in the early stages. It can even stay with you for the rest of your life, and you will be highly prone to experience another burnout much faster than it took the first time.

These days people dramatize everything, so as soon someone is a little stressed for a few days they call it burnout. If they have a headache, they call it a migraine. When they have a cold, it is the flu (or will we call it COVID-19 from now on?). You get the point. Somehow we have reached a point in society where we only receive help, support, and understanding when we are suffering from the worst of the worst illnesses and injuries. And of course, other times we are seeking validation or recognition when we share the dramatized version of our reality. We all want to be seen and heard.

To help you understand what a real burnout looks like, I will share my own experiences, including what got me there, what it looked like to be there, and what got me out. This is not medical advice. But, as I have been in consistent medical treatment for my chronic illnesses, much of what I will share here is information I received from my own doctors as well as what I have researched extensively myself.

Herbert Freudenberg, a German psychologist, was the first researcher to publish a paper with the term "burnout" in 1974. Though burnout has been acknowledged in some countries since then, it was not officially recognized by the global medical community until May 2019, when the World Health Organization officially classified "burnout syndrome" in the ICD list as a legitimate medical condition. Burnout is not new, and it's not a millennial phenomenon, although the millennial generation is certainly very outspoken about this topic, for reasons you may come to understand as you read the coming text.

Let me start with this: Burnout is a bitch. Yes, you read that right.

My burnout kicked in about 18 months before I realized and addressed it. 18 months. In those 18 months I could have saved myself A HELL OF A LOT of trouble. But that wasn't the plan.

It all started when I was an overambitious 22-year-old team manager, trying to turn that Siemens Enterprise Networks' crisis project around, save 160 jobs, and improve their working conditions. Within a year I checked a lot of the boxes. I took on 3 different roles, working harrowing hours, even 36-hour shifts, rotating through night and early morning shifts, all while sleeping no more than 4 hours most nights.

There were other boxes I ticked off, too, that I wouldn't have known to check a list for. I experienced a great deal of discrimination for being both young and female in the IT industry, and as a leader within it no ess. Then there was plenty of prejudice for the fact that I was born in East Germany. I was ridiculed and even bullied for my looks, which didn't align with the stereotypes of the "typical woman in tech."

Out of all of it, the most disturbing thing I had to deal with was sexual harassment. This is a subject that is not discussed enough, if we talk about it at all. It is a taboo topic, especially in male-dominated industries, where women are told to "grow thicker skin and sharper elbows." In other words, to pretend it didn't happen, because it wasn't that bad after all, it was just a misunderstanding, and now you're just making a scene, acting out, and making a big deal out of nothing. Be quiet, smile, and wave.

Maybe it was because I was young and naive, or maybe it was because I believed that as a team leader I had something to say, but I didn't just smile and let them harass me. I used all of the power I had, or believed I had, and I spoke up. To the men that harassed me, to my boss when I reported them, and to my peers on the team in the hopes they'd understand. That didn't always work as intended and got me in some extra trouble, but it also helped me gain some more respect and awareness and at least reduced some of the attempts.

Despite all of these obstacles, I smashed every assumption about me and surpassed every expectation anyone had about the results I could (or couldn't) deliver. How did I do this? I simply outworked everyone.

Fast forward to my second year in the company, when I was switched to a new project and forecast to become the new operations manager. This meant I would skip ahead and uplevel to my boss' current position in the leadership team. My ambition kept me excited about the new project, even though I knew I'd miss my old team, who had come to love me and appreciate the value I brought to the table. But the second year was the hardest one yet.

It started with me taking on too many roles, again. Surprise. As you can see, I had no idea how to set boundaries in the workplace, so it was easy for everyone to unload all of their work onto me, and they did. I quickly learned that the role I was initially promised wasn't going to be given to me. Instead, it was given to a woman who had worked for our client for a number of years, but had never been in a leadership position before.

This woman manipulated her personal connections to secure a transfer from Spain to Berlin, and then told the company that she would only accept a leadership position. She was offered a supervisor role, but when she learned there was a higher position (the one that was supposed to be given to me), she spoke to the client who she knew personally and demanded that they hire her instead. It was a behind-the-back political game and I didn't know how to play.

I was switched back to my original role as team manager, working underneath this new woman as the operations manager, but the game didn't stop there. Over the next seven months I was used, misrepresented, and bullied constantly. I was given more tasks than I ever had before. It was absolutely impossible to get all of these tasks done. I had a week's worth of tasks on my list every day, and I'm talking about the German ideas of "daily" and "weekly" tasks which is already its own level of insanity. When I wasn't able to fulfill the unfulfillable, my new supervisor would badmouth me in front of the client.

Next, she then started turning my colleagues against me, playing these power games with as many people as would play them. Since I didn't want to, she played with others, turning even more people against me. It didn't take long for the first signs of burnout to show up.

The medical and psychological fields recognize many different models of burnout syndrome, consisting of 4 to 12 or even 15 stages. These are the seven stages I experienced, which may or may not align with these. For me, the first stage of burnout, after the excitement, ambition, and devotion to the job faded, was filled with doubt.

1| The stage of self-doubt. One of the side effects of being bullied and gaslit, as I was at the hands of my female boss this time, is that you begin to doubt almost everything. Your work, your ambitions, your character, and even what you ate for lunch. I started doubting whether I was being treated unkindly or if it was actually me in the wrong.

I knew I was doing a great job, a phenomenal job most of the time, but the first year without a break wore me out. I could feel that I was getting tired, but I was told to work full hours nevertheless, which in this case meant 6 a.m. to 10 p.m., six days a week. I asked for support, and I was not only denied help but also made to believe that I was being weak and oversensitive for needing help. Slowly but surely, I started to question whether I was actually doing such a great job, or if I was indeed needy, weak, and not resilient enough for the position. I started doubting every step of my day, every decision I made, and also everything that I was being told.

2| The stage of feeling stuck. I don't usually need much sleep. I wake up early on my own and go to bed fairly late. But at this point I was tired. It was getting harder to wake up and get out of bed. My body felt heavy, my brain was foggy. I wasn't thinking as quickly and clearly as I used to.

I pushed harder. This is the only thing I knew how to do, and I wanted to overcome the doubt I was falling deeper and deeper into. I know I wasn't doing anything wrong, yet I kept getting in trouble, called into meetings, and called out. This could be for failing to get all of my tasks, my colleague's tasks (who was out sick for 8 weeks), and my boss' tasks for the week all done in one day. Yep. In one day. Or it was because my team didn't achieve their monthly sales goals by the end of the second week. If you want to find something to complain about, you will.

At this stage, I felt like I was giving in. Giving in to the games she played, giving in to the seemingly helpless position I was put in, giving in to the constant fatigue that was turning slowly into exhaustion. I was stuck. And I felt like there was no way out.

It felt like an eternity, but this stage probably lasted a few weeks. Meanwhile, the sick colleague eventually quit and I was left alone as a team manager on the floor. I swiftly slipped into the next stage.

3| The stage of frustration. In hindsight, after years of being frustrated over the smallest things, I now know that frustration is only damaging to one person: myself. At this stage of burnout in my career, I was frustrated just thinking about having to go to that damn job. I was frustrated by the way people drove cars, talked, walked, thought, and even chewed. I was frustrated at the slightest inconvenience.

I was most frustrated about my boss. Her unbelievable audacity to keep pushing her toxic agenda, and the many people who were too ignorant or blind to see her games for what they were, were especially frustrating. So much so that it started to creep into my mind a little too deep. I started talking myself into worst-case scenarios. I got frustrated at the smallest things my boss would say, and at my friends when they would question my perception of her bullying. Yet I still didn't clearly see the toxic environment for what it was, and since I couldn't put a finger on it, but I was still trapped inside it, I got frustrated.

The frustration made me angry, and this began showing up as the very first physical symptoms of burnout. I started grinding my teeth; I had muscle tension; tiredness turned to exhaustion; I was restless, my mind endlessly chattering; I woke up throughout the night from overthinking, stress, and nightmares. From this point on, mental symptoms became extremely physical.

4| The stage of physical manifestation. All of the stress and bullying and overwork began to show up in my body. It was so obvious that it felt like my body was screaming at me. This should be the last-ever station on the burnout train, and the time to jump off. Unfortunately, I didn't.

At first I was too exhausted to get up in the morning, but then I was in too much pain. Everything took an exorbitant amount of time. The muscle tension in my neck, shoulders, and back felt like a raging fire. If it wasn't for the high pain tolerance I had built up over the course of my life, I would have been on medication all day long. As I continued to work my 16-hour days, 6 days a week, with no end in sight, I became desperate for a doctor or an osteopath or anyone else that could help me with this pain.

I held onto the stress, frustration, and anger for way too long and it spiraled into a nerve inflammation in my shoulder and neck. At this point the pain was so bad I had no choice but to be on strong medication, even with my pain tolerance.

5| The turning point. I reached the next stage, my turning point, the morning I fell asleep behind the steering wheel of my car while driving to work. I woke up when people honked at me. At the time I was waiting at a red light, but the incident shocked me so much as this could have easily happened while I was driving too. This was my wake-up call to do something about the situation.

I knew that the constant bullying, tip-toeing around my boss, unreasonably hard work, and now the nerve inflammation had contributed to me being so exhausted that I fell asleep at the wheel. Realizing that my job had such a tremendously negative impact on not only my thoughts but also my health and my life in general devastated me. I knew that I needed to change this immediately.

6| The stage of desperate action. As soon as my boss came into work that day, I asked her if I could finish my shift and go to the doctor. She said no. When I asked what day I could go, she told me that if I got sick I would be risking getting fired. This is illegal in Germany, and I was shocked, but not surprised. I knew I needed to help myself in some way. I knew that if I would run into even bigger issues if I didn't take immediate action. In this stage of burnout you are frantically trying to turn the tide. Unfortunately, it is usually a lost cause at this point.

In my desperation, I started educating myself on my symptoms. I called my doctor and talked to him about what I was experiencing and asked for advice. Yet the experiences of the past few months and the threat of losing my job if I got sick put me in paralysis. I was torn apart about what to do, but it only took a few more days for my body to decide for me what I should be doing.

7| Collapse/Burnout. It was one of those days. Long, frustrating, full of painkillers and anti-inflammatories. My boss had plenty to say about me and seemed to enjoy defaming me in front of my whole team. I got home late after the long shift, opened the door, walked into my flat and put my bag down. BAM. A sound, as if a shelf full of books had crashed to the floor, echoed through the room as I broke down in agony.

"FUCK. Fuck Fuck Fuck. This is fucking painful. Oh my gosh, I can't breathe. Wait, don't cry. This won't help. Doesn't make you breathe any better. See that's what happens when you let people like this b*tch get in your head. Who even cares about her? Fuck. Well, apparently you, and now look at you, lying on the floor like … okay stop it. So. What is that? What's going on? Let's see."

These were my first thoughts as I laid on the floor. I was unable to move. The pain I felt was like lightning, moving from the top of my spine down to my bum and into my legs, then bouncing back up to my brain. It felt like I was paralyzed.

There I was. On the floor, motionless, in absolutely unbearable pain, hardly able to breathe, and with no one around to help me. I wanted to cry, but I couldn't. I also was afraid of breaking something in my spine. I laid there while I tried to make a plan. I'm good at plans, remember?

"Ok, let's think this shit through. Looks like your options are, well... limited. Ha. The fact is, you need to go to a hospital. I don't wanna dramatize this, but this sounded like some of your discs prolapsed in a big bang. So. Yeah. Get it together and get your ass to the hospital."

I took some deep breaths amidst gasping for air on the floor. I walked myself over and over and over again through the steps I needed to accomplish in order to receive help. Only 3 steps. Relax the muscles. Breathe. Get to the phone in my bag, somehow. I repeated the steps in my head while trying to stay calm and prevent emotions from taking hold of me. There was no way I would cry. Once I was a little more relaxed I made another plan. I would push myself forward with my feet slowly until I could reach my handbag. Then I would roll slowly onto my belly, move my left arm until I could reach the phone, and finally call for help to get to the hospital.

"Alright, great plan Monique, but how are we getting there? Call an ambulance. Hell nah, you know how useless they are. Hm, yeah. Katja? Hm. Well. She can drive. She could come and drive your car. Ok, let's try. You just need to get your phone and call her."

The hospital informed me that the "physical manifestation" of my burnout consisted of 4 prolapsed discs, including one that cut off my spinal cord, paralyzed my right leg, and caused the most torturous pain that I have ever had to endure. I also had severe nerve inflammation in my neck and shoulders.

This is what severe clinical burnout syndrome looks like.

Let's talk about how not to get here.

SECTION 2.1| BURNOUT PREVENTION

Burnout prevention should be one of your highest priorities as a leader. Not only is it a form of self-love and self-care, it is also an expression of care for others and responsibility and ownership. Setting boundaries can be one of the most powerful ways to prevent burnout. It isn't the only tool you need to do so, but if you set strong boundaries and stick with them, it can save you. Because of how important they are, there's a whole section on boundaries in chapter 7.

You've probably heard the saying, "you can't pour from an empty cup. I honestly never used to resonate with it, and I used to think it was such a silly saying. This says a lot about my own boundaries, or my lack thereof. To be honest, I still think this saying is a little silly, because I don't pour tea from my own cup into yours. I make a pot of tea and share it. But you know what, that's just me being extra German about it, so let's forget about it. I did eventually come to understand the saying anyway, right after my last job in Germany.

I don't believe that working too long, working too hard, or working overtime without days off for weeks or months on end is why people burn out. These conditions will probably affect your health and wellbeing at some point, but they may not burn you out. They can. But there is a much bigger cause than any of that.

The truth is that people burn out because of the people they are working for, working with, or constantly surrounded by. There, I said it. The emotional and mental burden people carry from being bullied, discriminated against, ignored, unacknowledged, and unsupported is what destroys people from the inside out. That's what burns us out.

This dynamic can show up in many different ways. Maybe it's your boss that bullies you and plays social and political games against you, like it was in my case. It can be colleagues who isolate and discriminate against you. It can be pain-in-the-ass clients that treat you like a servant. It can be patients that are nasty and cruel. Or it can be the caretaking of the people you work with or for, who might be sick or close to death, that impacts your mental health and physical wellbeing. There are so many different paths to burnout.

We learn early on to suck it up. We are told not to make a scene, not to cry, not to speak up, not to cause a problem, not to have our own opinion, and so on. Many of us take it to heart, and when we get a job, we do exactly that. We don't tell our boss that their bullying is bullshit, we don't tell our colleagues that discrimination is a lame form of insecurity projected back onto us, and we don't ask for support. And when we do, we may be sent away.

If we want to prevent burnout we need to be aware of our surroundings, of our role within the environment we move through, and of the way in which we are impacted by the people around us. Are there any underlying issues that you can identify that would be helpful to address early? Are there assumptions that you are making about others that may not be true? Address it. Clarify it. The best way forward is always transparency and communication.

One of the most obvious ways to detect and prevent burnout is by monitoring our energy levels. In Chapter 7 we will talk about "energy efficiency" more thoroughly, but I do want to mention it here because it's so important.

First we overlook our low energy, and then we pretend our energy is low for so many other reasons. We blame ourselves for eating the wrong foods, drinking too much soda, staying up too late, watching energy-draining movies, talking to the wrong friends, arguing with idiots on Facebook… I can keep listing all the excuses we find for ourselves when our energy levels are low for an extended amount of time. But what we forget to mention is the truth that low energy levels are the very first signs that we are on the way to burn out.

I'll say it again, loud and clear: If you feel tired, exhausted, low on energy, drained, unfocused, indecisive, scattered, forgetful, and you feel this way more often, more intensively, and in more consecutive days than you usually would, this is the very first sign screaming in your face that you need to slow down!

Yes, low energy can be a sign of many other things, too. Yes, I understand it can indeed be a symptom of physical issues. But I will dare to say that many of those very same physical issues also manifest from stress, overwork, and swallowing emotions. They start just like burnout does. So why not take the foot off the gas while you can?

I know I could have saved myself a hell of a lot of suffering if I did. If I stopped for a moment by the time I felt tired and exhausted (remember, that was already in the first stage of burnout, the stage of self-doubt!) and if, instead of doubting myself, I removed myself from the situation and made a plan to get out of the worn-down state I was in, I am sure I would have been able to get myself out of burnout. Without the big bang.

When my clients come to me, they are often already a few stages into the development of burnout. Then we have to repair instead of prevent. I promise, prevention work is way easier than repair or recovery work, if you start early. But it only works if you stick to it.

Preventing burnout is a daily task. Think of it as a check-in rather than a chore. I developed a daily 5-minute review that I integrate into my daily planning session. This helps me be brutally honest about my current state of being and prevents me from overlooking anything again.

In this daily review session, I ask myself the following questions:

- What was a win you achieved today?

- What was a lesson you learned today?

- Was there anything you worried about today?

- If so, what & why?

- Was there anything you would have changed about your interactions today?

- If so, what and how would you have changed it?

- Rate your average energy level from 1 (super low) to 10 (super high)

- Did you:

- Sleep well last night →

- Drink enough water →

- Eat healthy →

- Move / Stretch / Dance →

- Laugh →

- What are 3 things you are grateful for today?

These questions only work if you are completely honest when answering them. The review can help you see when your energy is low over an extended period of time. I wouldn't worry about a few days, but I'd look into it when your average energy levels stayed below 5 for longer than 10 days. Energy levels will swing here and there throughout the day, so it is important to answer these questions daily, and with an average of your all-day levels. Furthermore, if you keep writing the same thing under question 3, there is something cooking there. Speak to someone that is not involved in the issue who can offer an outside perspective and maybe some advice on how to approach the situation. Do not drag it out.

If you have neglected the 5 daily habits of well-being for a while (sleeping well, drinking enough water, eating healthy, moving, and laughing), there's a good chance it's not because you simply decided you ain't doing this shit anymore. There's probably a root cause of your neglect hidden somewhere that needs to be found and addressed. It's often because something on our minds is making us anxious, stressed, or depressed, or else keeping us so busy that we simply forget to take care of ourselves. Addressing this as early as possible will help prevent a big bang, whether burnout or other health issues.

In summary, here are the three main elements that we need to pay attention to in order to recognize and prevent burnout:

- Boundaries

- The people we are surrounded by

- Energy efficiency

Outside of these three considerations, there is another issue at play that many leaders struggle with, which can often lead to burnout on its own: perfectionism.

SECTION 3| Perfectionism

As a recovering perfectionist, I can tell you that trying to be perfect has been one of the most harmful and limiting behaviors that I have engaged in personally and witnessed in others.

I sure did, and still do, have many flaws. Since childhood they were used as weapons against me, so I became a master at hiding them. At the surface, I seemed perfect. I was great at everything I did, even the things I tried for the first time. I was the fastest runner in my school, even faster than 99% of the boys. I was great at soccer. I was even good at construction, because my dad had a construction company and I helped him build houses and repair anything that needed fixing. I could change the tires on my car. There was no need for me to ask for help from anyone. I was so perfect. And, unconsciously, I let everyone know.

There are so many reasons why this can be so detrimental, but to mention a few, I

I believe, and studies have shown, that the root of perfectionism is low self-esteem due to early childhood experiences of blame, shame, punishment, and a feeling of not being good enough. I had plenty of all of that. The first time I remember feeling "not good enough," and a burden to everyone around me, was at the age of three. It is my very first memory, and though it was a happy moment at the time it later turned into a negative memory because of how I perceived what happened. Looking back, this was the moment that sparked my inner perfectionist and shaped the trajectory of my life.

You might be thinking, "Well, I do like to get things right, but I am certainly NOT a perfectionist. That's a bit over the top." If that's the case, I want to help you see what being a perfectionist looks like. Here are some typical scenarios:

- Getting stuck in planning and preparing tasks, but never actually taking action because things are never perfect enough

- Talking yourself out of anything and everything because you are never ready, never good enough, never prepared enough, and, well, just not perfect

- Talking everyone else around you out of their own pretentious ideas because "can you imagine that someone could take imperfect action?" Pfft. Please.

- Constantly thinking self-defeating and outright bullying thoughts about yourself and shaming yourself for stupidity as soon as you dare to think something positive

- Being anxious is your default state

- Being chronically stressed is your default state

- Developing jealousy for people further ahead than you, and looking down on people who do dare to be imperfect, take imperfect action, and make mistakes

- Constantly comparing yourself to everyone in every possible scenario, even when it makes no sense whatsoever

- Correcting everyone around you to the point of absurdity

- Feeling personally attacked when receiving feedback

Sound familiar? Yep, I promise you most of these things were on my own list up until a few years ago, when I worked through them one by one. I found that perfectionism gave me a lot of safety, and it was a great way to cope. When anything went wrong I told myself that it must be my fault. Maybe it was because there were so many things going wrong all the time, it thought it had to be my fault. Or maybe it was because I was told that everything was my fault so often that I eventually believed it.

Perfectionism is destructive. It's destructive to your mind, your soul, your health and your relationships. And besides that, it doesn't even work. It will not make you perfect. Because here is the irony behind it all: There is no such thing as perfect.

Perfectionism, at its barest definition, is *the need for other people to see you as perfect because of insecurities about oneself and the fear that other people will see these insecurities and flaws in you.* To break the cycle and step out of perfectionism, we need to address the following list one by one:

1| Let go of the need to be perfect

If you want to recover from perfectionism, the very first thing you need to understand is that perfection is not a goal to have on your bucket list, and it is not achievable in any lifetime.

It helped me a lot to paint a picture of what being perfect would actually look like. I thought about having to keep up a perfect look all day, a perfect smile, to always be in the perfect mood (what does that even mean?), have the perfect relationship, the perfect business, eat the perfect food (that's where this desire started crumbling for me, no donuts? Wow.), wear picture-perfect outfits... the list goes on. After an hour of listing all the perfect things I had to do and be I was so drained that I couldn't even imagine how draining and stressful it would be to keep up all that perfection in real life. Uh, NO. Thanks.

I looked at my list and wondered what it would be like not to be perfect in most of those areas. And guess what — I was able to make peace with it. After a while it even felt freeing. Many of the qualities on my list were social norms, like what it means to be "on time" in Germany. I calculated how much time I had wasted by arriving at appointments 15 minutes early just because it was deemed "polite" to do so. Hell no. From that day on, I was *on time* on time. I walked in the second I was supposed to be there, and no sooner.

2| Give yourself permission to be imperfect

Once I had made peace with the idea of imperfection, the next thing I had to do was give myself permission to actually *be* imperfect. Sometimes I still need to do this, like when I'm late to a meeting or appointment because I felt sick, or got stuck in traffic, or had to get gasoline, or I forgot about it… you know, because I was human. I used to hate myself for mistakes like this. I'd talk down to myself and run red lights, putting myself and others in danger just so I could be perfectly on time. Now? No way. I give myself permission to be human. Now, I send a message to let everyone know I will be late, apologize, and then show up safe and sound with my best, un-stressed energy.

But how do you give yourself permission to be imperfect? Well, you can simply say, "Alright, you do not have to be perfect at this. It's absolutely okay to make mistakes. It's okay if you don't get it right on the first try. You learn while you do it." Sounds silly? Cool, the first step to embracing imperfect is to do something you think is silly, so give yourself permission for that, too. As you recover from perfectionism, a lot of things will sound or feel silly and weird to you, especially in the beginning. That's okay. Let them be weird.

Ask yourself: Is there anyone in the world that you seriously expect to be perfect? If so, why?

3| Dismantle blame, shame, and guilt

Addressing shame and blame will be an ongoing topic for you as you recover from perfectionism. One of my absolute favorite books about daring to be imperfect is *The Courage to be Disliked* by Ichiro Kishimi and Fumitake Koga. It uses the principles of Adlerian psychology to deconstruct the ways our emotions influence our actions, and talks about how to free ourselves from the need to be perfect so we can truly be ourselves and achieve happiness.

The very best way that I found to deal with blame and shame was to learn the difference between what is your fault and what is your responsibility and to adopt this difference into everything you do.

If something is your fault, then you are the direct cause of an incident. In one way or another, you triggered or influenced a situation with your choices. Your actions caused a particular event to happen. Importantly, that means that nothing that happens outside of yourself is or can be your fault.

For example: You punched a wall and broke your fingers.

That is your fault. You chose to execute a punch with your bare hand and your target was a brick wall. Your choices were the cause of the outcome. The outcome was a few broken fingers.

Responsibility doesn't look at the cause of a situation. It's all about the result. Talking responsibility means being accountable for the outcome of a situation, and for your choices, feelings, and actions, even in situations that you did not cause.

For example: You had a fight with your partner. It got heated; your partner punched a brick wall and broke their fingers.

That is not your fault. But it is your responsibility now to be accountable for the situation, including how you feel about it, how you respond to it, and how you grow from it so that next time the conversation will have a different outcome.

A lot of people would feel guilty about their partners' broken fingers. But you didn't take their hand and punch it into the brick wall. And I assume you don't know how to telepathically make people do things that you want them to do. In that case, it is not your fault. It was solely their decision, choice, and action. It's *their fault*. All you can and have to do is take *responsibility* for your side.

In short, taking responsibility means finding solutions and learning lessons from the results of situations so that future results can be improved. Applied to our perfectionism, this looks like examining every situation in which we feel like we have done something wrong. We need to take every incident we think we messed up, or issues that we think are our fault, and take a quick assessment:

1| Was this really my fault? Did I actually cause this situation?

- If yes, what can I learn from it and how can I make sure to not repeat it?

- If not, what is it that I need to take responsibility for?

2| How can I make sure to turn blame, shame, and guilt into responsibility?

3| What do I need to understand the situation and detach myself emotionally from it?

Working through blame, shame, and guilt is no joke. It will be an ongoing task. When I take my clients on this journey, we go step by step through this exercise and these assessments. The logical breakdown helps to see and understand the situation clearly. And once we can see clearly, it becomes easier to dismantle blame, shame, and guilt and move forward productively by taking responsibility for all situations in your life and business.

Perfectionism is rooted in deep insecurities that are based on blame, shame, and guilt. We use these painful feelings as the foundation of negative stories we create about ourselves. These feelings are often planted early on in our childhood, and we carry them long ways through our lives until we consciously look at them and decide to break them down. We have to break through walls of blame, shame, and guilt in order to let go of our need to be perfect.

4| Let go of control and trust yourself

This is the hardest one for many people. Many of us don't even notice how much of our own lives we want and try to control.

We try to control other people's feelings and opinions about us, our impact, the time, the traffic… hell, sometimes even the weather.

There is no way we can see and deal with our control issues if we continue to try and control everything.

Being called a "control-freak" felt like a compliment to me for the longest time. I thought it showed me that I had "everything under control." This is just as laughable as being perfect, though. There's no way for us to control anything outside of us, and trying to do so will have uncomfortable or painful consequences. Burnout is one of these.

Letting go of control was probably the hardest part of this process for me, and quite honestly, it still is a challenge in certain areas of my life. I always believed that I had to control everything in order to make anything go right. Spoiler alert: it didn't work.

Instead, the more I tried to control everything, the more everything turned into a mess. Then I had to figure that mess out, and try to control the mess, and suddenly it's a whole damn hamster wheel of control. Once I stepped out of that spinning wheel or, more accurately, once I was catapulted out of the spinning hamster wheel of mess, I realized I was missing the one thing I needed to actually make things work: Trust.

Ouch. I didn't trust myself. This is why I wanted to bend everything else around me to my exact liking. See, I have always had a very deep (though hidden) faith that I can achieve anything. I guess that's why I have achieved so many extraordinary things in such a short amount of time. But *trusting* that I was doing the right thing? Ugh, nah. Somehow that slipped out of my survival kit.

When I talk about faith and trust in myself I mean two completely different things. They seem very much the same at face value, but there is an important difference.

Faith in oneself is a deep knowing that one can achieve anything and get through everything. It is a conviction that cannot be shattered and does not need proof or validation. I believe everyone is born with it and has it deep inside, but for many people it is buried under layers and layers of society's expectations, rules, restrictions, rejections, blame, shame, and guilt from the day we are born.

Trust in oneself is the belief that we know better than anyone else what is best for us. It is the ability to choose the right thing, even if it is the hard thing, because we know it is what will keep us safe and fulfill our needs. It is being kind and compassionate with ourselves while also being 100% honest and true to oneself, in order to grow and move forward.

So how did I start trusting myself after years of being told I couldn't, I shouldn't and that it'll all go wrong if I do? After decades of blame, shame, guilt, being told that I was a burden? Through the belief that I shouldn't "make a scene" (which is to say, have my own opinion) or else nobody would love me?

I had to jump. This looked like a lot of different things. Letting go of control and trusting yourself go hand in hand, which is why it was (and still is) the hardest part for me.

When I first started this process, I had to ask myself a series of clear questions when I made every decision. What should I do? Is there a gut feeling I can base my decision off? Why would I question it? Who would have been the person to question this decision and come up with "a better one"? My mother? My grandparents? My teacher? A friend who thought they knew better?

The most relevant question was, "What does my gut say?" What was my intuition, the first thought that came into my head? No matter how silly, weird, or even frightening it sounded, I forced myself to follow this thought as often as possible. When I didn't, it would come back. First like a whisper. Then it would nag me like a mosquito bite. Finally, I could hear it screaming at me. I had to do it.

This happened with decisions like ending a relationship I knew I shouldn't have gotten into to begin with. It happened when I first thought about quitting my job and leaving Germany, but it took me another 3 years to actually do so. It goes back farther than that. If we count from the first time I heard that whisper in the back of my mind telling me to leave Germany, it makes 11 years between when my gut told me to leave and when I actually left. I was 15 years old when something inside of me told me I didn't belong there, but I didn't act on it. Maybe because I was too young, or maybe I had been told for too long not to listen to myself. Whatever it was, I didn't listen, but the whisper only got louder. It kept nagging me, so I moved to London for a short time after my cardiac arrest, but returned home again. I still had a lot of excuses left, so I stayed. The voice in my head got louder and started screaming. I negotiated as much time off as I could to travel far from Germany twice a year. It wasn't enough. On my last vacation, as far from Germany as possible, the screaming finally hit me. When I came home I quit everything and packed up my life. It took me six more months to leave. There were still lessons for me to learn before I could go.

I now fully understand that you only have two options: either trust yourself, no matter how hard it is, or learn a lesson from not doing so. And sometimes those lessons are so painful, you'll wish you had just trusted yourself in the first place. As you rebuild trust in yourself, it is helpful to examine your environment, your relationships, and the way you think about and speak to yourself.

4.1| Language - How do you think about and speak to yourself?

Oh, language. I can not stress enough how much language matters when it comes to changing your patterns and building strong trust in yourself. I used to have a lot of voices in my head that constantly judged me and weighed in on everything I said and did. Two voices were the most prominent. I called them my inner Drill Sergeant and my inner Ballerina. They certainly didn't agree on anything, so the "discussion" about me in my head was ongoing, loud, and stressful.

The Drill Sergeant voice tore me down, talked down to me, made me feel bad about myself, shamed me for my ideas and decisions, and questioned everything I did. He speaks German and sounds like a dickhead. You know, one of those people with no good intentions, probably an insecure man who puts you down to feel better about himself. The amount of guilt and hate, swearing and shame that the Drill Sergeant berated me with would have been enough for three world wars. I listened to this intimidation for decades. And I took it all in.

As I shed layers of my past I came to understand that this voice was a combination of family members, teachers, and fake friends. It was every put-down and insult I heard from everyone around me for my entire life, burned into my brain in the form of the Drill Sergeant's voice.

The Ballerina speaks English. I learned English in primary school from the age of 7 onwards and spoke more or less fluently by the age of 19. I loved being able to speak other languages, and I felt like English especially was a secret language. The Ballerina's voice was graceful, always gave me the benefit of the doubt, and encouraged me. It was strong and powerful yet light as a feather. She stood up against the Drill Sergeant like a marine and never backed down. The Ballerina won the battle, but it took us A LOT to get the Drill Sergeant to shut up.

www.moniquelindner.com   @themoniquelindner

But how did The Ballerina and I do this?

First, I had to understand that not all of these voices are *my* voices. The Ballerina clearly was. I danced ballet for 11 years. It is my heart and my soul and deeply ingrained in who I am. This voice is me.

By contrast, I am absolutely not a drill sergeant. I can speak like one, I can play the character of one, and I have been told that I would make a very good one. But still, it is only a role. This voice is not me.

We need to be able to identify the voices in our heads and understand where they come from. Not everybody's inner voices are a Drill Sergeant and a Ballerina, but I believe everyone has had similar voices in their heads at some point in their lives. Let's call them the Hater Voice and the Cheerleader Voice.

Once I identified my Hater and Cheerleader voices, I had to set up a cycle-breaker to be able to interrupt the pattern. I chose to say "Stop", "Shut up," or "No" to my Hater voice. This has to be said out loud. You can also use a code word, like "durian" (it is the stinkiest fruit in Southeast Asia), in case you are out and about and surrounded by people. Then you can say this word out loud without people being too concerned. They might be a bit confused, but don't worry. We wanted to practice letting go of control, right?

Every time your Hater Voice comes up with some thoughts trying to tear you down you say one or all of these out loud. Once, twice, or three times.

"SHUT UP!"

Now that you've interrupted the thought in your brain, you want to plant a new thought. It should be the opposite of what just came up for you. For example:

Hater Voice: "Are you serious? You want to put this shit in this book? Who do you think wants to read this bullshit? I mean, damn, this is the crappiest book I have ever read, and you are writing it. Shame on you."

Cycle-Breaker: "STOP. SHUT UP."

Cheerleader Voice: "Alright my friend. Let's not listen to this, that is NOT correct. The truth is that people need to read this book. They need this because you are writing from your heart and telling your Truth. There's no shame in that, and I promise, so many people will relate and be relieved that someone put this out there. Now let's keep writing, 'cause this stuff is magical!"

(This may or may not be an actual conversation I had quite often in my head about this book. So, there's that.)

Changing the language we use, even in our heads, can help us change our perspective. And changing our perspectives can help change our paradigms. And once we change our paradigms we can achieve anything.

4.2| Your friends, family, and other people around you

Uh oh. Now we're talking. This is and will be a big thing each and every time you are leveling up. Take a good look around you. Who do you talk to a lot? Who do you share your daily struggles, progress, wins, and challenges with? Who are you surrounded by? Just assess the top 5 to 10 people. Ask yourself, how do these people react when you fail, make mistakes, or have down days? How do they react when you win, make progress, or get to the next level? And how do you react when the situation is the other way around?

Look at the patterns. Are there friends who talk down to you? Do they keep trying to fix you when you just need someone to listen? Are there people who are always there when you fail but don't cheer when you win? Are there people who are always there when you win, but go missing on your down days? Look out for these people. These are the ones you need to confront and ask for an upgrade.

I understand that not every friend can and will be a friend for "everything." We all have people to talk business with that ain't the right people to talk about our private lives, and that's cool, as long as they are there for you during the good, the bad, the ugly, and the champagne-bottle moments. The same goes for your friends on the more personal side of things.

Look out for the people who use your relationship for its benefits but don't give back, people with behaviors that feel toxic to you, and for people who show patterns of jealousy, lack of support, or anything else that doesn't feel safe. This is completely subjective. What feels safe to you does not need to feel safe to me. Certainly abusive behavior patterns are an exception, which need to be acknowledged and addressed.

We practiced letting go in the previous step, but that time it was just about control. This time it will be different, as we may have to let go of people. We can still love and support someone and have to let them go in order to grow. Sometimes we have to do this in order to leave our own toxic behaviors behind. Sometimes we have to do this more than we'd like to.

In my life I have let go of more friends, close acquaintances, jobs, family members, communities, and sports groups than I could line up around a soccer field. Twice. There have been a lot of people. It was painful, and still is, each and every single time. Until you get to the other side and take a deep breath of relief. First, you might feel a bit of shame for feeling relieved, but then you'll just feel relieved for shedding a heavy burden that you carried with you for probably way too long.

What happens if the person you need to let go of is a family member? Hm. That's a really tough one. The way I did it was a slow, step-by-step process. I started off in consistent contact with them, sharing my thoughts and opinions about the parts of our relationship that harmed me. When that didn't work, I gradually removed myself from our conversations and, later, from meetings with them. Finally, I removed them from my social media completely and clearly expressed that I was no longer interested in a relationship with them.

There were a few family members with whom I cut contact without hesitation, and told them immediately and clearly that I was not interested in any further interactions. This choice and the boundaries surrounding it were not respected by one very close family member, and it was an ongoing struggle and challenge for many years to get the distance and non-contact that I needed to move forward with my life.

A lot of people believe that "blood is thicker than water." This phrase is merely a free ticket for abuse. We stay for way too long in way too many awful and abusive families just because of the "thicker blood." I say it's bullshit. For starters, our bodies are about 60% water, and our blood is about 50% water, so there's that. Besides that, another version of the expression is "the blood of the covenant is thicker than the water of the womb." Family bonds are not necessarily stronger than other kinds of love or friendship. Know that you can opt-out.

You can choose and create your own family. Your family can consist of friends, colleagues, people you are helping, mentors, leaders, communities… There are billions of people in this world. You will certainly be able to create your own family, whatever that means to you.

And yes, for some of us it is absolutely possible to love our family members from a distance. We do not always need to completely break relationships off. There are many different versions that can work for you. But if you feel like you need to leave one or more of your blood family members, then leave. Don't wait. Listen to the Cheerleader Voice telling you to walk, walk fast, run if you must.

4.3| "How you do one thing is how you do everything"

As we make progress in gaining trust in ourselves, letting go of relationships that do not feel good for us anymore, and using more positive language to speak to ourselves, we need to learn how to be consistent.

Consistency does not just mean we do one thing repeatedly until we accomplish a goal. Consistency also permeates other areas of our lives and businesses, showing us the patterns that run deep in our systems. It's exactly what the title of this step says. Whether you like it or not, "how you do one thing is how you do everything."

Does that mean that if you skip your workout this morning because you are too tired from being awake all night with a crying newborn that you will skip it every morning? No, I don't think so. But if you don't work out at least a tiny bit at some point in the day or evening to make up for the one you missed, then you could set yourself up to break the exercise habit that you've built. Now you've given yourself permission to miss the workout when you have a "good reason."

And does that mean that if you go to bed late tonight because you had to meet a deadline for a client that you will go to bed late every night? No, I don't think so. Unless you use the late bedtime as an excuse to also scroll through social media for another hour and watch meaningless videos online. Now you've given yourself permission to repeat this behavior by not treating it like an absolute exception for special work circumstances.

There are correlations between following through with one decision and following through with another. If we plan to take an ice-cold shower each morning, and then do it, we are far more likely to sit down and work on our difficult tasks for the rest of the day. Both are uncomfortable, and it would be easy to chicken out with some kind of excuse. But if we do the first uncomfortable thing (like an ice-cold shower), we are way more likely to do the second (the hard work).

Our brain connects our emotions, feelings, and thoughts about every task and will register our next actions based on our previous decisions. Once we break the chain and decide to not do the first thing, our brain starts building a new neural pathway for that decision to reinforce a new "habit" (even though we don't want it to be a new habit) and will repeat the behavior in search of the dopamine hit of approval. The next day you will end up having a new excuse, and another one the next day, and then at some point you've already stopped taking ice-cold showers in the mornings, so why bother now? After a week or two, you'll start seeing this creep into your daily work habits. You'll see yourself making excuses for things. You'll need to push way harder to the point of forcing yourself to do the most difficult tasks... until finally, you miss a day.

So how do we reverse this? Action. Yep, there's no other way around it, you literally just gotta do it. Choose the least uncomfortable task out of them all, say the ice-cold shower, and just do it. Just start. You can take small steps. Take a 30-second cold shower for the first week, and increase the time until your full shower is ice-cold again. But do it. And don't even try to get it perfect. That's the whole point. We're leaving perfect behind.

4.4| Spend time alone with yourself

This one must be my favorite step, especially for my clients. I have gone through this step so many times, and I know that each time there is so much more to learn.

Being alone with yourself—and I mean truly alone: just you, no other people, no telephone, no social media, no internet, no work, no tasks, nothing to be busy with—is one of the most challenging things for us to do. But it can be, and often is, incredibly freeing.

See, our brain hates boredom. It truly does. Once it gets bored it goes back into its default mode: survival. Since we no longer live among saber-toothed tigers and dragons, our brain now has to come up with some other clever shit to keep us busy. Imagine if we weren't busy all day and actually spent time alone? We'd have to face our deepest darkness that bubbles up from the hidden corners of our inner selves. Doesn't sound fun, does it?

So what does the brain do when we get bored? Create drama. That's right. Our brain creates situations that we need to "survive" from. It gives us problems and challenges and issues to solve, all so we can get away from the darkness. When you are alone, your brain can't do that, unless you trip over your own feet and break both of your arms. In all seriousness, though, when you are alone and unplugged (and if possible, in nature), with no distractions for long enough to get to a state of boredom, you can't escape it. And you shouldn't. This is exactly what we want. This is only the beginning, so stay with me. Or in this case, with yourself.

The key is to listen. By this time you may or may not have practiced ignoring and transforming your Hater voice into a Cheerleader voice. You want to hold onto this practice when you're alone. Listen to everything that comes up, all the suppressed feelings and emotions. Sit with them, then start writing it all out. You don't have to keep it. You can burn it later, or you can drown it, rip it apart, whatever feels best. Whatever you do with it afterwards, writing it down is an act of letting go. Of acknowledging it and getting it out of your system. Once you read back your words you can start the work that is coming up between the lines. For that, I highly recommend looking for support.

Being alone gives you the opportunity to practice everything in this section in one sitting. Set a goal to be alone with yourself for 14 days to start off. You'll get better at it over time, in one way or another. You'll certainly learn a lot about yourself. You'll learn to trust yourself more (if not fully), to hear and handle the voices in your head, and to keep promises to yourself by doing each thing the way you want to do everything. Spending time alone with yourself is the ultimate "let go and trust" experience. It strips away perfectionism, because there is no place for perfect between you and you. That's the point.

Unlearning perfectionism has a lot to do with leadership. In Section 1, I shared 11 key traits that I believe every modern leader must embody. To be able to embody these traits, it is absolutely necessary to leave perfectionism behind, trust yourself, and be able to be alone for an extended period of time. It's very common for leaders to come from backgrounds that created a need for perfectionism. It's time to dismantle this now in order to truly step into your role as a modern leader.

SECTION 4| Core Values

Defining your core values is one of the most powerful tools for leadership. Core values are the principles and beliefs that are of non-negotiable importance to us. We lead our lives and businesses with these values, sometimes unconsciously. If you like to define your top 3 to 5 core values, you can find a process to do so in the book experience at www.thetimemethod.com/bookexperience.

We often claim that oh-so-many values are important to us, but the truth is that there's usually only a handful of principles that we hold onto no matter what. When going through the core value exercise with my clients, they often get stuck in the last round where they have to prune a list of about 30 values down to the last 3 to 5. They simply can not decide which ones to choose and which are less important. I ask them one question that puts the exercise in a whole different perspective.

"If you were kidnapped by secret agents who said they'd kill you if you didn't give up on your values, which of these values would you still hold on to, and which ones can you let go of?"

With a question like that, most of my clients immediately drop 20+ values. Not because they are not important at all, but they are simply not non-negotiable.

Having non-negotiable core values in your life and business makes your direction clear. It becomes completely clear to you what decisions to make in times of crisis and even when simple issues arise. It is also clear what you need to do for others, how you show up, how you live your life, how you react when being challenged, and so on. For every situation, your core values are the answer.

If that sounds too simple for you, maybe it is. Yet even Albert Einstein allegedly said, "The definition of genius is taking the complex and making it simple." So, to make it as simple as possible for you to understand, I'd like to give you an example. Let's say your core values are kindness, honesty, and courage. Here's a possible scenario:

You are an inclusive fashion brand creating super fun active wear for everyone in every size, and you are looking for new ambassadors. Your brand clearly asserts your core values and you talk about human rights issues on your social media, including LGBTQ+ rights, Black Lives Matter, refugees in need, and other pressing issues of our time. You are using your brand as a vehicle for the impact you want to make in the world.

In the weeks you spend advertising your brand's new ambassador program, you receive a ton of messages, even some from influencers in your field. You are so excited. There is one particular influencer you've always wanted to work with, because you love their style and their message. You get in contact, start a conversation, and decide to send them the digital contract for the program. The contract stipulates a fine for either party should they bail out of the deal for no reason, unless any of the company's rules of participation have been breached.

Two days after they signed the contract, you see comments from this influencer on another person's profile. This person whose profile they are commenting on happens to be a trans woman. The influencer got into a heated discussion with this trans woman about a political topic in the comments section, and is now using derogatory language to call the trans woman terrible names. What do you do?

Let's reframe this question. At this moment it is not important what you would like to do. Instead, you need to ask yourself these three questions:

> What would Kindness do?

> What would Honesty do?

> What would Courage do?

When you have the answers to all of these questions, you will know exactly what to do. In this case, I believe it would look something like this:

- Send the influencer a kind (yet firm) message to let them know you have seen these comments. *(courage)* Ask them to connect on a call. *(kindness)*

On the call:

- Share your core values and explain what these mean *(kindness)*

- Share what standing up for human rights issues, in this case LGBTQ+ issues, means for the company *(kindness/honesty)*

- Admit that you may not have done your research well enough/didn't share these values clearly enough/whatever else comes up in the conversation *(honesty/courage)*

- Let them know that you can not move forward with a brand ambassador who uses this kind of language, especially against people whose rights your company is fighting for *(honesty/courage)*

- Offer a solution to the contract *(kindness)*, or make the contract void for specific reason *(honesty)*

- Share what you will change and what actions you will take so this will not happen again *(honesty/courage)*

- Ask the influencer what lessons they will take from this experience *(courage)*

That sounds like a calm and mature conversation, but it may not necessarily go like that in real life, especially with someone who has already used derogatory language on an Instagram post. So be prepared, and lead from your values: Kindness, honesty, and courage.

When we define our core values, we suddenly have clarity about the hardest conversations, the most uncomfortable tasks, and the most difficult decisions. They do not become less difficult or uncomfortable when we have to execute them, but our direction is absolutely certain. It removes all doubt from the situation and it helps us to develop deep roots in our being.

SECTION 5| Leadership From Within vs. Leading By Example

I want to finish this chapter off with the distinction between two leadership styles, one of which is very popular. As we have seen, a lot of good leadership has to do with you, the way you treat yourself, how you take care of yourself, and how you show up for yourself. Your actions for the collective, whether it's a team or your family or a community, will always reflect what's going on inside of you. Remember, no one needs to be perfect, and no one wants to see a perfect leader. But we do need a leader we can relate to, one who comes from our playgrounds, one who knows what they're talking about, and one who will fight for us even when there is no direct benefit for the leader themselves.

The two different leadership styles I want to talk about are "leading from within" and the more well-known kind of leadership defined as "leading by example."

1| LEADING BY EXAMPLE

This style implies that not only do you know what and how to do things, you also do them yourself. You walk the talk, so to speak. This sounds good, but it opens you up to a few potential pitfalls as a leader.

For example, if you are trying to show your team how to work hard, but your actual understanding of "working hard" is to hustle for 15 hours a day (which I hope, by this point in the book, is not in your mind anyway) all you'll do is burnout the team.

Another example could be creating a team culture that feels like a family but everyone still takes their work seriously.

"Leading by example" will cause you to create a culture that feels closest to what this experience would look to you. But your team members may be from different cities, regions, or even countries, and might not feel the same way. This means that creating that team culture definitely must be a team effort, and "leading by example" could do more harm than good.

On the other hand, leading by example comes in handy when you define your core values and truly live them day in and day. When people can see these values shine through your decisions, language, actions, and everything that you do, then leading by example will be a great way to convey these values to your team so that they can successfully carry out your company's mission.

I don't think we should dismiss the "leading by example" style but rather make moderate use of it, and only when the outcome is beneficial for everyone involved. Whatever you do, be sure to walk the talk, lead by example, and then move out of the way. This is where the second leadership style comes in.

2| LEADING FROM WITHIN

This leadership style is everything we've talked about so far and more. Leading from within takes the person you are speaking to into account. It says to "treat everyone the way they would want to be treated". I recently heard that quote from Tayo Rockson, a living example of what it means to "lead from within." Rockson tells us to treat people the way THEY want to be treated, not how we think they should want to be treated. To do this, we need to call upon some of our 11 leadership traits from Section 1, such as compassion and willingness to be a student, in order to hear what someone is saying, understand what they need, and then apply that to our own behavior in the moment.

"Leading from within" is set up to ensure that you are bringing your best self to the table and including the person or people you are working with. It is building a big enough table and bringing all of the chairs so everyone has a place at the table. It also means inviting each and every person to the table by name, instead of saying, "everyone is invited." Leading from within is removing ego from the game and replacing it with compassion, trust, and understanding.

The difference between leading by example and leading from within may seem rather small but in the long run it makes a huge difference. It's all about the ego. In this case, ego isn't negative, but rather more like Eckhart Tolle describes it. "The identification with thinking becomes ego. Which means simply that you believe in every thought that arises and you derive your sense of who you are from what your mind is telling you who you are."

Does that mean a leader who leads from within does not have an ego? No, we all have an ego. But the leader who leads from within knows that their ego does not have a place in leadership. It must take a step back in order to bring out the best for the collective. When leaders lead by example instead, they sometimes get stuck in their pride about how things are "supposed to be" done, or can't let go of control of "doing it their way." They can miss out on important lessons because they can't see the opportunities that lie along different paths and approaches.

Leaders who lead from within, have learned these lessons already and are willing to let go of the ego during the period of the day that they spend in leadership. Or, when a situation triggers a response from their ego, they are aware and can address it.

Should this part of the book trigger you or elicit any resistance, then I probably hit the nail right on the head. I will close the chapter with another Eckhart Tolle quote. "The ego cannot dissolve itself but in the light of awareness it dissolves."

So let's be aware.

CHAPTER REVIEW

Check in with yourself to see what emotions come up after you have read this chapter. If you feel some resistance, breathe into it and see where it comes from.

Here are a few action steps for you to follow:

- Where do you stand with your own leadership? Do you prefer a certain style that you were taught?

- Are you a leader by example? Why or why not?

- On a scale from 1-10 (10 = I am right there), how close are you (honestly) to burnout? If you feel like you are already in the process of burning out, what stage of burnout are you in?

- Do you believe you are a perfectionist? Which of the steps from Section 3 can you start implementing today?

- When was the last time you checked on your core values? Head over to www.thetimemethod.com/bookexperience and find your top 3-5 core values. Don't forget to share them with us on Instagram and tag @themoniquelindner so we can celebrate with you

Mindset Mastery

My clinical death awakened a will to live in me that nothing and no one could ever take away. Before the death, during the migraine attacks, seizures, and weeks of endless agony, I would sometimes silently and secretly wish it would end. Not in a cute way, where a fairy comes down to magic it all away. No, I mean—

Maybe a seizure would make me drop in front of a car and—

Or that an attack would strike while driving and I'd run my car into a wall so hard that it would—

Sometimes I wished that I could just end this myself and—

—and everytime I had a wish like this, the next thought was, "Shut up! You don't actually want to die. Like this shit is insane, I know, but man... I want this to stop, now, please, like, make it stop! But don't you die!"

I never told anyone about these thoughts because, quite frankly, I thought my cardiac arrest and clinical death was my fault. I thought that I had wished to get out of this shit one too many times and had finally got what I was asking for. I thought I caused it. And, in one or another, I did. I did get myself to that point by overworking, under-sleeping, using work to cope with trauma, plus quite a bit of alcohol on the weekend that surely didn't help, plus liters of coffee a day (more coffee than water). I was never tired, though. Until I burnt out years later, I was never exhausted. There was no sign. I just dropped dead. Quite literally.

In hindsight, the signs were screaming in my face. I just didn't see, hear, or feel them. I was coping. For about 25 years that's what I did to survive day after day of excruciating physical pain that slowly but surely crept into my mind and spirit. How can it not? When you don't learn to process you will cope instead. But coping only helps you for so long. What got you to this point won't get you any further. In fact, the very thing that saved your life before, may now be holding you hostage.

My coping mechanisms saved my life, and they almost killed me.

They saved my sanity, and they almost drove me insane.

They pushed me through the hardest moments of my life, and they also triggered some of the very same moments later on.

Duality. There is no day without night. There is no sunshine without rain. There is no calm without the storm. The moment we grasp and internalize this concept, we will be able to develop what I call stoic strength.

Stoicism is the philosophy of resiliency. In its original meaning, it aims to leave suffering behind through clear judgement, emotional intelligence, and logical reasoning. Whether that's the only way to go about it is a question for a dissertation.

What stoic strength means to me is the understanding that only through life's duality, through the light *and* the dark, will we be able to know our true capacity, test our will and devotion to life, and grow, one challenge at a time.

Resilience and stoic strength does not mean that you are fearless. It does not mean that you do not go through rollercoasters of emotions, or even that you don't want to throw in the towel at times. No. It means that in the same moment you pick up the towel to throw it in, you look at it and wonder what towel animal you could fold out of it to make the moment a tiny bit more enjoyable.

You accept what is and then make the best out of it. You transform pain into power. Suffering into striving. Obstacles into opportunities. That is resilience. And stoic strength is when you do it every time, again and again, and you know why you do it. And how.

The first time I got a glimpse of this was when I was five years old suffering from a 7-day migraine episode. At this time, the only medication I received was painkillers delivered as a suppository. Don't look at me like that—I didn't choose that delivery. I promise, I would have swallowed the biggest pills they had but no, the doctors preferred to do it that way. I will save you the details, but I will say that this was the start of me not trusting doctors. Because "no" obviously didn't mean "no" and "I'd rather swallow that big ass pill" didn't mean anything from a 5-year-old.

So instead of "no" to the medicine, I'd just say nothing at all about the illness. I started hiding my migraines. Or so I hoped, because hiding when you have to puke as a child isn't that easy. But I learned how. I trained myself to suppress the puking and blend the pain into the background. Let's not talk about whether or not that was healthy. It was certainly a coping mechanism. But it was a stoic process I went through, and I was only five years old.

At five, I certainly didn't know that what I was doing was called "stoicism," but it worked, so I kept doing it. I got quite good at practicing this. At times I was able to hide my migraines so well that I would forget about them myself until they hit me so hard I fainted, or collapsed in the classroom, or suddenly started puking in the middle of dance class.

Besides the unwanted suppositories, I had plenty of reasons to hide my migraines. So many people had so many different unwanted opinions about me and about my illnesses. For more than two decades, they told me:

- I made it up in my mind (whatever I was experiencing)

- I was just playing the "sick child" to get attention

- If I was truly "so sick," why wasn't I at home?

- I was such a burden to the family, it would have been better for them if I wasn't around

- I made my family's life so hard. Every time they wanted to go somewhere, they had to leave because of me. (This one never came from my parents or sister themselves. Funny how other family members can make up things like this.)

- No one will ever love me if I am always so difficult to handle

- It's not fun to be around me because there's always something wrong with me

- "Why don't you just (insert useless advice here) if you feel *that* bad?"

- But you don't *look* sick!

I am not sharing all of the bullshit people told me (really, just a fraction of it) so that you pity me. Please, keep pity to yourself. I also don't share this so that you gaslight yourself into thinking, "damn, my problems ain't that bad, so I shouldn't feel XYZ about them." No. I'm sharing a tiny bit of the challenges I faced as a child because I want you to see what is possible, and then go do it. I want you to know that people are not born with these mindsets. They are not born with a set of tools. They learn, practice, and repeat them thousands of times. They develop and then test them by being thrown into real-life challenges.

In short: You can do that, too. You can achieve whatever it is you want to achieve. The only thing holding you back is your mind. So let's shake it up a bit in there, shall we?

SECTION 1| Motivation Is Bullshit

Motivation is bullshit. There, I said it. Now that that's out of the way, let me explain what I mean and what we can do instead.

Motivation is not an external influence that will get you out of bed and make you want to do hard stuff. It's not something you can go and buy when you run out, like coffee beans. Motivation is not a state of being or a feeling as such, but rather an action. When people misunderstand the function of motivation this way, using it to talk about how they feel in the moment, they are not able to actually reproduce it.

So how does motivation work? As Dan Wieden so wonderfully campaigned for Nike, "Just do it." Maybe that's disappointing to you now. And that's okay.

Indeed, motivation is the result of discipline, action, and consistency. Instead of motivation itself, we need to create a steady flow of actions by developing the first line of offense in the form of persistent goal-completion. We need to attack the task before we are motivated to do it. We need self-discipline.

I have to be honest—I don't see much discipline in the world these days. I don't mean the punishment version of discipline, but rather the self-discipline that makes you proud after you work long and hard to achieve something. Or the kind of discipline that makes you train for years and years and years to get to the Olympic Games. Whether you win a medal or not, just getting in is a huge win by itself because of the immense discipline it requires. Self-discipline comes with long-term gratification. So screw that dopamine kick you get from your daily Stripe and Paypal notifications. It will not help you develop discipline. "But it's a great motivation"... back to the bullshit.

I learned discipline early on. As a child with two chronic illnesses, there was always a lot to take care of. Be here and go there, get to doctors appointments on time, take medicine at certain times, don't eat certain things. Even though my parents took care of a lot of that, I certainly soaked up all of what was going on and a lot of that responsibility became ingrained in me.

But the real hardcore discipline I learned came with becoming a ballerina. I was three and a half years old, just after my life-saving kidney surgery, and I dove in headfirst. I wanted to be the best, not just "really good." I needed to be Number 1. Not just because I loved dancing so much, but also because I seemed to be no more than a burden everywhere else. Being a Ballerina gave me the chance to be truly great at something, and to be wanted for it. So I went all in.

I'd dance day in and day out, no matter the pain, the challenges, or the struggles. My love for dancing was bigger than everything else I needed to endure in order to achieve my goals with regards to ballet. Discipline became my best friend.

Discipline is getting up in the morning at the time you planned, whether or not you "feel like it" or it is "too cold outside" or "you rather want to spend the morning in bed with your partner."

It's eating healthy meals every day, every meal, no matter how much you are craving a burger.

It's going to bed 1 hour earlier because you know it will do wonders for your health, even though you'll miss your favorite TV show.

It's saying no to shiny objects, no matter how glamorous and full of glitter and unicorns they are when you know they are only a distraction.

It's taking days off to rest, rejuvenate, and recharge when everyone around you is working through the weekend and looking down on you for not doing so.

I would describe discipline as *the consistent act of showing up for yourself in the best possible way, doing the right thing instead of following distractions, and dismissing instant gratification for the reward of a long-term goal.*

These are the steps I found most important to the process of developing discipline.

1| Start

Looking at all of you perfectionists hiding behind the book! Seriously, if we don't start we ain't getting nowhere. It's like typing a destination into your GPS, packing your bags, getting in the car and then just waiting for it to get there by itself. Maybe in the next 10 or 15 years Elon Musk can help you with that. For now, you gotta drive to your destination yourself. That means you also gotta do that damn thing yourself, whatever it is you're putting off. Get started!

2| Grow into love with the process

I don't quite believe in "falling in love." I believe we grow into love instead. This is a state of being rather than a feeling. Grow into love with your journey. Whether you want to become the best scientist in your field, or the most sought-after speaker in your industry, or the highest-paid writer in your niche, be in a state of love with everything that comes with the process. The light and the darkness, the highs and lows, the struggles and the wins. Grow into love with every single step of the way to your goal.

3| Stick with it

Through the lowest lows, the stickiest stuckness, and the trickiest tests, you gotta stick to it. Yes indeed, there are times when it's better to let something go, and when that time comes you will know it. But if that time comes, it doesn't mean that letting go of that one thing means letting go of your path. Being good at something does not come from trying it once or twice and letting it be when things get hard. No, being great at something comes from repetition. You have to repeat it often so that you dream about it and you could do it in your sleep. And then some. To make it stick, you gotta stick with it.

4| Learn to say "No," and say it often

There will be many distractions and shiny objects along the path. There will be people who try to drag you down and keep you small. Developing discipline requires a certain awareness of these obstacles. Learning to say No has been a life-saver in this regard. Make "No" your second-best friend (after discipline itself).

One of the best pieces of advice I ever got was that I do not owe anyone an explanation of why I am saying no. For example, it became clear to me at some point that many social gatherings were energetically draining for me and, to be honest, not enriching in any way. At first I had a very hard time saying no when I was invited to events I didn't want to attend. I filled my calendar with other commitments just so that I could say I was busy.

I had to learn how to say "No." It was a process. First I learned to say it at all, and later I learned *how* to say it. If you can already do both at the same time, amazing. If not, just start with saying it. Do it right now. Say "No" out loud about 15 times. Now I just say "No thanks" or "Maybe next time."Not only does that help me to stay on my path and strengthen my discipline, it also reinforces my ability to stay disciplined. I don't just jump off my chair to chase after every shiny object that crosses my path. Saying "No" keeps me on track with my goals, and that loop gets stronger the more you reinforce it.

5| Know the difference between procrastination and self-care

Uh, oh. This is a big one. First, know that I am not anti-procrastination, but so many people just don't know how to properly utilize it, and they end up simply wasting time. It could be busywork, scrolling through social media, staring out the window too long, getting lost in unnecessary research, or whatever else is your favorite way to procrastinate. Maybe your thing is cleaning and other household chores because "no one else is doing it" and "it must be done."Yeah, sure.

Self-care is different. Self-care means prioritizing, acknowledging, and taking action on our needs in order to protect our physical, mental, and emotional health. It could be sports, getting our hair done, getting a massage, seeing friends, taking time alone, reading, or walking in nature. It looks different for everyone, but it's all important.

When we work a lot, self-care can make us feel guilty. We also get self-care confused with procrastination, and then blame ourselves for not working hard enough, or taking "too much" time off (not that I would know…). We engage in self-care out of self-love and empowerment, but we procrastinate out of fear and insecurity. And here's a plot twist: sometimes we also use our self-care practises to procrastinate. And sometimes we do things that are definitely procrastination but we disguise them as self-care in order to hide from the truth. Yeah. That's a thing, too.

Now, before we hop into the rabbit hole of guilt, let me tell you that it is okay! It's okay to need time. It's okay to procrastinate. As long as we are aware of it, we can utilize it. But if you want to build discipline, you must be fully honest with yourself. Learn to recognize when you are actually taking care of yourself and learn to admit when you are procrastinating to get away from discomfort.

Here's the thing. I am all for fun and glitter and glamour and chasing unicorns. Life is already serious enough, why take it so seriously on top of it? But if you do have big, hairy, audacious goals (you know, like climbing Mount Everest next year with just twelve months of prep) then discipline is and should be your best friend. Motivation will come with it, just like that.

SECTION 2| Resilience Is Key

If we're talking about mindset, then resilience must be in the conversation. Resilience is typically defined as the ability to bounce back or recover quickly after hardship or crisis. To me, resilience means so much more. I believe that if everyone had enough resilience, the world would be a much better place.

To understand what I mean, I want to share what resilience is not. I see so many people, especially in my field, telling the world how "resilient" they and their clients are. I promise you, they are not. Don't let them fool you with their fake "I am strong" masks. Resilience has nothing to do with being fearless, suppressing emotions, or being strong in its toxic form, which involves looking away from pain and hurt. Resilience does not involve harming others in order to make yourself look better, feel better, or stand out. Resilience also has nothing to do with toxic behaviours like ignorance, the silent treatment, name-calling, harassment (in any form), or gaslighting.

It is quite the opposite.

Resiliency starts where all of this toxic bullshit ends, with processing hurt, pain, and suffering and growing through them. We can't heal from pain if we don't acknowledge that we have been hurt, remember? And even when we do, that's only the beginning of a long road. Resilience can only be built when we take full responsibility for our lives, and when we maintain an attitude of gratitude for the lessons we have learned through struggle. And that is often not very pretty, or at least not until we get to the other side.

This doesn't mean that we have to be positive, overly enthusiastic, or fake happy all the time. I tried that. It's not only hella exhausting, but it also doesn't work. At all. You can add this to your list of toxic behaviours. This is one of the hidden ones, one of those that are accepted by society because "being positive can't possibly be harmful, right?" Wrong. Fake happiness can certainly harm you, and it can even harm others depending on how much we overdo it and how the others take it.

I know that taking responsibility for our entire life is a hell of a task. I know that the ugly times don't beg for gratitude. But I also know that not a single one of the wrecking balls that crashed into me and my life, again and again, harder and harder, left more than a scar. This is because I developed resilience from a young age, and I was grateful for the lessons each and every time, even if it took me a while to get to this point.

So let's look at the steps it takes to develop resilience. These may not be the complete, A-Z blueprint, but I promise that implementing these steps will improve your resilience.

1| Take responsibility. 100% of the time.

Self-responsibility is holding yourself fully accountable for your response, even when the issue is not your fault. I learned this lesson in so many different ways. Here are a few examples of what it looks like to take responsibility—100% of the time, in any scenario, and no matter what. These are all examples from my own experiences and, although I won't explain them further, I will say enough for you to understand the context and impact of them on my life.

- I was involved in a car accident with three other people, including the driver. I sat in the right back seat of a 3-door Audi. The car who drove into us came from the right side, ran a red traffic light, and crashed into the part where a door would have been in any other kind of car. The other three people in the car got away with minor injuries. I ended up with a lifelong spinal injury, neck trauma, and several other follow-up injuries. I was 15 years old.

- I was about to be kicked out of school and had been called into the director's office for the 3rd time. This was my last warning. She told me I wouldn't be allowed to finish my high school degree (which would have prevented me from going to university) because I kept falling asleep during lessons and the teachers complained about me. She put me on a 1-month probation period and told me that if I fell asleep one more time or missed one more class, I was out. She didn't want to hear the reason I was falling asleep or missing school. On top of going to school full time, I was working 3 different jobs to support myself (my dad had lost his job 3 years prior and was now in school to start his own business). I had been taking 2-3 different antibiotics for the past 9 months because I experienced regular renal bed infections and UTIs, on top of my normal migraine medication. I was 16 years old.

These examples all have one thing in common: It was not my fault. None of it. Not a single bit.

These examples have one other thing in common: My choices brought me to exactly the places that I needed to be to experience these things.

This does NOT mean that I asked for it. It does NOT mean that I attracted it, or that I was unconsciously looking for it to happen. Forget all of this "law of attraction" stuff that may be coming to your mind now. That's not how this works.

What I'm talking about is simple cause and effect. If I had chosen not to go to the Cheerleader Trainers Event that weekend and be tested for my training licenses, I would not have had that car accident. But I DID choose to go, and we DID have that accident, which also meant that I never finished my training licenses. Not because of the accident, but because of the effect that the accident had on my health, my life, and my mind. At that point, I chose not to finish.

Here is where responsibility comes in with all of these 3 examples:

The car accident took a lot out of me—physically, mentally, emotionally—and it sucked the energy out of my soul. Everything but lying on my side and walking slowly was a nightmare for more than 3 months. I was only excused from school for a few days. I have never really missed school or work for being ill. It's just not done in Germany, or so I believed. So I pushed myself through ALL of my duties no matter how much pain I was in, even when I couldn't stand or see or speak. I just trained myself to do so. I went to school with my wrecked spine and stood in the back of class for 8 hours a day because I wasn't able to sit. I looked for a physiotherapist to help me in any way I hoped they could. I researched my own rehabilitation methods and did them at home, daily. That is, when I wasn't in school, or work, or doctors' appointments, or side jobs, or meetings for the sports team that I captained.

Was that the healthiest choice? Absolutely not. But I made no excuses, no "I can't do xyz because of …", no finger pointing. Nor did I feel sorry for myself about 85% of the time. Responsibility in this case meant not drowning in self-pity and doing the best I possibly could with the situation I was given and the knowledge I had or was able to acquire in a short time.

In the second scenario I wasn't even given the chance to explain my situation to the school director. I was told I was the cause of my issues, wrongly blamed, and given the consequences. But I was also given a chance. A small one, but I took it. It took every ounce of me to be on time, attend every class, and stay awake. Between my full time job after school and two part-time jobs on the weekends, I don't remember when I did sleep or how I survived this time 9well, until I didn't).

Taking responsibility in this case meant changing the way I did things. It meant drinking more coffee (which was no small accomplishment considering how much coffee I already drank). It also meant to get rid of the antibiotics, which meant I had to get healthy in the first place. At this point, I was wrong about the root of the issue, so the healing took longer, but I took it upon myself to find supportive natural remedies to speed things up. I also took responsibility in school to be more communicative, informing teachers when I was ill and hence not very energetic, which saved me a few more complaints as they thought I was tired from working or partying.

Both of these scenarios could have been an invitation, especially for a teenager, to blame the rest of the world instead of taking responsibility for my own actions and taking care of myself.

This is natural. In any situation where something happens to us, without us being the cause, we tend to feel like the world owes us something. Some kind of special support, redress, or at least someone else to take care of the uncomfortable parts of life that we now have to deal with. Or that we "at least" can use the situation as an excuse for those days that aren't going well and the times that we feel moody or like a victim. Because frankly, we have been a victim. But though we may be a victim of our circumstances, we do not have to stay in the mindset of a victim.

On the days when we want to hide—when physiotherapy sucks, when people are frustrating to be around and someone is pushing you out of the way and hurting you because your slow walk with your injured spine is too slow for them— these are the days that we need to take full responsibility for everything that has happened no matter who caused it. These are also the days that it sucks the most to do so. And these are also the days that force us to grow the most, when we will develop resilience.

Certainly it can all be a turmoil of feelings at the same time, which is the next step.

2| Feel all the feels. Then let them go.

This only took me about 3 decades to understand and internalize, which means it finally clicked for me not that long ago. I was fantastic at feeling and releasing happiness and anger, and the process looked the same for both: I danced. Or I'd drive my car really fast on the Autobahn, screaming along to music on full volume (to say "singing" would be an insult to the many incredible singers out there, so "screaming" is a more accurate explanation). The only difference was the kind of music. Rammstein for anger, Coldplay for happiness. What took me 3 decades was learning the difference between other emotions, how to identify what emotions I was currently experiencing, what other feelings they translated to, and why those feelings stuck around even when the emotion that triggered them was gone. So I studied it.

The scientific difference between emotions and feelings is the level at which they take place. Emotions can be conscious or subconscious. They are a neuro-physiological reaction to our circumstances that we experience as a physical sensation. Oftentimes these are facial expressions as well as sensations like a pit in the stomach, a frog in our throat (not literally), blushing, or our heart skipping a beat. Feelings, on the other hand, are experienced consciously as a result of our emotions. They are only experienced on a mental basis, even if we believe that feelings can hurt.

This means that one of our basic emotions comes first, which then triggers a feeling based on our subjective experience of this emotion. Once I understood that, a whole football stadium of lightbulbs went on for me. I had opened up a whole new Super Mario Super Level of emotional intelligence! We can *decide* how we want to feel based on the emotions we experience. This is mindblowing to me!

That pit in your stomach can be an indicator for "oh damn, something is really wrong here" or "whoooo this is super exciting!" It's your choice, and you can make that choice each and every time, depending on the situation.

That pressure on your chest can mean you haven't said something out loud that you want to but know you shouldn't, or that you need to relax more and take it easy. It's up to you.

Unlike our feelings, we can not decide which emotions we experience, and that's great. These emotions help us listen to our intuition. And, according to neuroanatomist Dr. Jill Bolte Taylor, the lifespan of the actual neuro-physiological reaction in our brain that makes up an emotion is only 90 seconds. We experience emotions like sadness or anger or happiness for longer than that because of the stories we attach to situations and the justifications we come up with in our minds in order to explain these sensations. We want to be "right," and we don't want to be the ones at fault for whatever went "wrong."

Once I understood the difference between emotions and feelings, the lifespan of an emotion, and that emotions were neuro-physiological processes that happened as a reaction to our circumstances, the next thing I needed to understand as a logical learner was, How do my brain and my body work together? Which physical reactions do I experience in what type of situations? What triggers can I find that repeat quite regularly? What happens as soon as the emotion is set into motion?

To be able to explore this, I had to detach my feelings from the physical sensation. This is not an easy task, but doable. Since I wasn't feeling anything but anger and happiness anyway, and I was so good at suppressing everything else, I probably had a bit of an advantage there. Or, let's just say I used it as an advantage. But everyone can practice this.

A great way to start is to set an intention while you meditate. Start with a body scan, then go into a visualisation of a recent situation that stirred emotions for you. Instead of attaching to the emotion, observe what happens to your body. Do another body scan. What's different? What came up during your visualization? What sensations came up in your body? Where did you feel them? Do they pass if you explain them logically to yourself?

The same process works in real life. Whenever emotions arise, Dr. Jill Bolte Taylor recommends taking a full 90 seconds to watch what is happening inside and outside of yourself, paying attention to how the situation is unfolding and the sensations that are coming up. She calls it the "90-second Rule," and it has 3 steps: (1) Identify the emotional reaction, (2) label the emotion, (3) allow the emotion to come without judgement, observe it, and let it pass.

Using logic to identify emotions, explain the sensations happening in my body, and the feelings I experience as a result of those sensations has been so useful to me. Detaching from these feelings and knowing I do not have to identify with them has helped me sit in them, be with them, and let them go without attaching justifications, judgments, grudges, and stories to them. Instead, I can just observe it, feel it, and let it pass.

3| Have hard conversations. Especially with yourself.

The first two steps won't help us move forward if we are not true to ourselves and the people around us. And being true to ourselves and others only works when we can communicate that truth. These kinds of conversations are everybody's least favorite, but the benefits of having them are huge.

- Everyone in these conversations will learn something, whether or not they are willing to do so

- Communicating during hard conversations is great practice for observing emotions and being able to let them flow without attaching to them

- Hard conversations will always create a win-win outcome as long as both sides are participating from a place of love and leading with good intentions, even though it may not feel that way

The reason we don't like hard conversations is pretty obvious. They challenge our capacity to be uncomfortable and speak our truth. They force us to admit when we are wrong in front of someone else without judging ourselves. We have to be willing to learn in the moment.

Meh. Doesn't sound like something on my list of "fun things to do on a daily basis."

But that list also doesn't contain "be a coward." And that's exactly what we are doing when we choose not to have these hard conversations. We are choosing to be cowards. Harsh? Yep. The uncomfortable truth? Also yep.

So I will take the first option and put "having hard conversations" on my "meh-things to do on a daily basis that are not fun but make me a better person" list. And I suggest you do too. Whether this means having a hard look in the mirror, or being honest with a family member who needs to look into the mirror, or having a hard conversation with a friend who is telling you uncomfortable things that you need to hear... These are the conversations that will help you grow.

4| Know that after a hurricane comes a rainbow—the duality of life.

> *"If you only knew what the future holds after a hurricane comes a rainbow"*

> — Katy Perry, *Fireworks*

Yes, you read that right. I just quoted a Katy Perry song, and I am not sorry. Look, we ain't taking life seriously over here, okay? Now that we got that out of the way, let's dance!

Katy Perry hit on A LOT of truth with this one lyric. She explained the duality of life, the dark and the light, the highs and lows, the storms and the calmness, the sadness and the happiness, all in one line. "After a hurricane comes a rainbow."

The first line carries even more truth. If only you knew what to expect from tomorrow, next week, or the moment 2020 finally announces the winner of the bullshit bingo and can vanish into the abyss that we call history… we would probably not be so stressed, anxious, serious, and freaked out about the uncertainty lingers all around us every day. Because, well, we would be certain about what was coming.

But then we would have a new problem: boredom. And we already know how much our brain dislikes boredom. So we'd end up creating even more chaos, drama, conspiracies, and overall bullocks just to make life a little more interesting. Can you imagine? More of all that than we have in 2020 already? I mean, I probably know enough islands to run to and watch this theatre from afar…

But in all seriousness, if we knew what was coming we'd go crazy. So we don't. But we do need to trust that things will get so much better after a shitshow like 2020! And that's the whole point. We can also trust that things will get way worse for the people who feel that 2020 was actually a success (yes, they exist, even though it's hard to believe…)

The most important part is cultivating a deep knowing of life's duality. It is up to you how high and how low you want to ride those waves.

5| Find the lesson that is yours to learn, and learn it.

Yes, and learn it. Ha, here's a lesson that I had to learn 100 times: Learn a lesson the first time

it is presented to you. Surely it is there for a reason. And by learning it the first time around I'll save myself a lot of time and energy, and oftentimes money and trouble. After all, this is still a book about time.

So don't we learn and adapt the first time a lesson is presented to us? Well, there are a few reasons, but the most obvious ones holding us back are cognitive biases. Cognitive biases are systematic patterns of deviation from rational thought. These patterns cause us to think and feel irrationally in terms of how we look for, evaluate, judge, use, interpret and remember information, and then how we make decisions based on these patterns. There is a growing list of cognitive biases, the longest of which is at 104. Our brain isn't actually trying to find the truth, it is trying to find ways to confirm our current beliefs, even if we do not like them. Tell me that isn't weird! Even weirder, cognitive biases work even when we are aware of them, and even when we try to suppress them.

In order for us to learn a lesson from an experience, first we have to find the pattern. Let's go through an example to see how cognitive bias gets in our way.

I loved eating spaghetti carbonara, yet the egg-parmesan mix did not work well with my stomach lining, which was highly inflamed due to hundreds and hundreds of doses of antibiotics. How long did it take me to learn the lesson? Thanks for asking. About 12 years. Yes. I didn't say 12 times eating carbonara. No. I mean *twelve years* of consistently eating Carbonara even though I knew it was the evil cause of severe cramps, stomach pain, and even vomiting, plus other consequences that often lingered for more than a week after I ate this meal. Twelve years, because a cognitive bias called "liking/loving tendency" made me simply ignore the fact that this meal would cause me so much pain. I loved my beloved carbonara so much that I was willing to overlook its flaws for twelve long years.

I didn't just stop eating carbonara. I ended up getting so sick with stomach issues for seven months that I had to radically change my entire diet, starting with a 10-day water fast. This was so difficult that I am just not willing to risk it anymore. No more carbonara.

You see, to overcome and change my bias, something extreme had to happen. My pain and suffering in general had to become much bigger than the pain of change, in this case not eating carbonara anymore. This is how I learned my lesson.

Not every lesson was this hard for me to learn. The biggest lessons usually came the fastest. This reason lies in the pain and suffering. The greater the pain and suffering one endures, the higher the chances one will change, as the pain of change will be less than the pain of suffering to stay in the same situation. .

This is the reason we see so many people who dislike or even hate their 9-5 jobs. We ask ourselves, "why don't they just quit and find another job?" But we know the answer already. The pain of staying in the job they hate is still smaller than the pain of change. Once that scale tips, they will endure the change. Which brings me to the next point.

6| Don't be afraid to change directions. It's the outcome that matters.

Change is the only constant in life. You have probably heard that many times, because it is true. If nothing changes, nothing evolves. Yet it is so difficult for us to change. We're always trying to keep things as they are. This is partly because of the cognitive biases we just talked about. They keep us in the same mindset and the same environment and make it hard to adapt to new beliefs. Pain is another factor. As humans, we are led by pleasure and by pain, and change is always derived from pain. The desire for pleasure can be a driving factor for change, yet it is pain that initiates the change.

But there's another thing that keeps holding us back from change: the shame and fear of changing our opinion, especially publicly. This often stems from the belief that if someone changes their opinions or beliefs, they are automatically untrustworthy. Because that means their previous beliefs and opinions were wrong, right? Why else would they change them now? And if they were wrong before, what would make them right now? That whole line of questioning makes us believe the person is no longer credible. And that in itself is wrong.

That was a lot of "right" and "wrong," but in short, we often discredit other people for changing their beliefs, opinions, or religious faith. We do this especially if their new beliefs don't fit into our own belief system anymore, or when those beliefs would challenge us to rethink our own current belief system.

This is also a reason why people struggle with change. Change challenges our belief systems and the beliefs of the people around us. If we change, it could mean that our peers no longer agree with us. If they decide that they don't align with your new beliefs and opinions, they might leave your inner circle. That would feel like rejection, and nobody wants to be rejected. But in order to build resilience, we have to have the courage to change. Change itself is inevitable.

7| After any challenge, get (back) in the game.

Rejection isn't the only thing we fear. We also fear failure, success (yep, that's a thing), imposter syndrome, and so much more.

Through everything I have faced in my life, one thing has always been crystal clear: I had to get back in the game. Resilience is built on the battlefield. It is not built in the comfortable warmth of your bed, nor is it built from behind the screen where you can send hate comments like a world champion keyboard warrior. Watching five hours of motivational videos on Youtube and walking over hot coals with Tony Robbins will also not make you resilient. Sorry to disappoint you. This is NOT how resilience works. I know, it's a shame.

Deep, ingrained resilience is built over time, with lessons learned, mindset upgrades, and lots and lots of practice. Practice is only cemented into skill when it's tested, which means you have to go back to the battlefield. I don't mean actually going to war; I hope we don't need to talk about that. What I mean is that you need to prove that you indeed learned the lesson, you uncovered the pattern, you changed the belief, you implemented a new behavior. You have to prove that you made the change. Not to anyone around you, not to someone on the internet, and not even to yourself. You have to prove it to your nervous system.

Your nervous system is the one that needs convincing, otherwise you will be tested over and over again until you eventually learn and finally implement the change.

Sounds familiar?

SECTION 3| Factual Thinking

My migraines started when I turned four years old. That's not an age where you consciously choose a particular way to deal with physical pain. You just do what feels best. Since everyone around me but my dad was more concerned about these migraines than I was, panicking about every attack, I decided to stay cool. Crying made the pain worse, talking made me more nauseous, and moving around wasn't an option since the migraines usually made me faint.

To be fair, the migraines were pretty severe and, with the addition of epileptic seizures, they must have looked very scary, especially when you couldn't do anything to make them better, except be quiet. Silence and darkness. These, however, were requests that didn't go over well with the people around me. "Well, we want to help you, but not in *that* way. Let's turn on the light and talk as loud as we can to make sure you understand what we want from you."

The older I got, the more I called for my dad when I needed help or to be picked up. He would send people away, tell them to be quiet, and let me be. He would ask me once what I needed and wait for an answer, even if it took me ten minutes to reply because speech impairment is no joke. My dad never freaked out, panicked, or made me feel like I had to calm him down. This is why I wanted him around, and still do. Even when he didn't know what to do, and even when he was afraid for me, I never knew it. I didn't have to worry about it while I was busy with, you know, having a migraine, with not being able to speak, see, move, or think clearly.

When someone else tried to help me, like my mum or friends who couldn't help but be shit scared and freak out (bless them) or be annoyed with me for having a migraine and seizures (yep, that happened a lot, too), my nervous system went into alarm mode. Having a panic attack while having migraines and epileptic seizures is no joke. The last thing you need on top of migraines and seizures is an overdrive of your nervous system. In order to stay calm and keep the extreme pain and the seizures as under control as I was able, I started calming the people around me down. I would ask them to relax, tell them nothing would happen, and that everything was going to be okay. I made sarcastic jokes, usually about myself. This was a coping mechanism, but it wasn't for dealing with my disease itself. No, it was purely a coping mechanism to deal with the projected fear, resentment, and uncertainty around me.

When these attacks would hit me out of nowhere, which they did for many years until I learned to read the smallest signs of them starting, I talked myself through everything that happened, step by step. This helped me to see "what is" and not make anything more or less of it. Just facts.

I stuck to the facts so that I would not attach any stories, any feelings about WHY this was happening to me. This was crucial for me to be able to literally survive. As a child, I would close my eyes and do this in my mind. Sometimes I would hold on to my plushy and whisper to it. I told my plushy what was happening, what I would do, and what I would have to wait for in order for the pain to go away. I also told the plushy what this was not, like cancer or something in my brain that was broken. I told the plushy that nothing was wrong with me. I repeated it so that I believed it.

Later in my life, this thought process saved me from depression, from becoming addicted to painkillers, and from trying to take my life when this was a very viable option. I call it factual thinking.

Factual thinking is the process of assessing a situation in the moment, stating the facts that we are aware of, and helping ourselves understand what we know, what we don't know, and what is possible to accomplish with the information that we have. It is a process of assessing the possibilities in front of us without fake positivity and potentially dangerous "everything will be ok" thinking. It is evaluating a situation without slipping into negative thinking. Instead of over-focusing on a problem, factual thinking finds a solution and a way forward.

Factual thinking is vital in moments of crisis. When we experience crisis, challenge, and trauma, our brain immediately turns on survival mode in order to navigate through it. The "flight-fight-freeze" response originally described by Walter Bradford Cannon is an acute stress response. It describes "a physiological reaction that occurs in response to a perceived harmful event, attack, or threat to survival." Depending on the level of stress or harm, our previous experiences, our cognitive biases, and our beliefs about the trigger, we may be prone to overreact in one of these three ways, moving into emotions like anger, aggression, anxiety, or panic. Factual thinking can help to better navigate these situations.

When I was in that car accident as a 15-year-old, I knew something was very wrong with my neck and spine. Yet, by talking myself through this event, going step by step through what is, what I know, what I don't know, and what I can do with that information, I managed not to panic.

When I double fractured my wrist as a 19-year-old, I evaluated the situation, assessed what is, what is not, asked for help, went to the hospital and endured the procedures without anxiety, panic, or freaking out… just a little impatience and frustration (I am laughing hard about the "little" impatience as I write this).

Factual thinking will help you get through every challenging situation, not just crises. It is useful in times of failure, stress, fear, illness, and even loss. It is the skill of sticking to the facts, without attaching stories to them that will create feelings. It will keep you from losing direction and keep you calm as you move through the challenge.

I am not saying you are supposed to suppress feelings or "just get over it" — I'm the last person to say stuff like that. Each and every time I used this technique, consciously or unconsciously, it got me out of the crisis situation safely, which in this case meant without creating more harm. I was then able to process it all after the crisis was over. Whether that was a car accident, a cardiac arrest, several life-threatening trips to the hospital, sexual violence, being a witness in court, losing my grandmother, fracturing my wrist, interfering in a dangerous fight, or any other situation.

Letting emotions and feelings take control of your brain in the midst of crisis can be harmful and sometimes even dangerous, to you and to others around you. Here are the steps that need to be practiced daily in order to develop factual thinking skills to help in times of crisis and challenge.

1| Stick to the facts.

The key to factual thinking is sticking to the facts. We've already learned enough about how our brain operates to know that this is the most difficult part. To be able to do so, we need to be able to ask ourselves the right questions, and know the right moments to ask them.

I was able to practice this when I traveled to Vietnam in 2012. I was walking on the side of the road towards my hotel, where I planned to meet a friend arriving from the airport. I pulled my phone out to text him the address. The moment I moved to put my phone away, a motorbike driver came up behind me, hit me with his bike, snatched my phone from my hand, and sped off. My first reaction: Run! I followed him through the traffic, yelled at him, and tried to catch up to him at a red light. I'm fast, you know! He saw me coming and drove through the red light into oncoming traffic. In that moment the loss struck me like lightning. I walked out of the middle of the street and stood on the sidewalk in disbelief. Another Vietnamese man asked me if I needed help, and I feel like I yelled at him, too. Poor guy.

I realized that if I wanted to handle the situation I needed to act fast and also clear myself of adrenaline. I walked myself through the facts. I asked myself what had happened, what the current situation was, what I needed to know, where I needed to go, and what I had to do so that all of my accounts, emails, and so on would be secured.

I walked quickly to the hotel, where my friend was already waiting for me. I told him to go to the room, as I would be busy for the next few hours taking care of the aftermath of losing that phone. Within approximately four hours, I changed all my passwords and informed my mobile phone provider, my bank, and every other institution in Germany that needed to be informed. I spoke to my insurance, went to the police and made a report, and went back to the place where it happened to see if anyone witnessed the incident.

I was only able to move quickly, secure my accounts, and potentially save myself from being scammed because I used factual thinking. If I let my emotions take over, I probably would have searched Ho Chi Minh City all night long for that guy, trying to track down that phone myself, cursing like a sailor in every language.

I did allow myself to feel all the feels and curse for a while, so I think I'm good on that, too.

2| Forget about "be positive" and "everything will be OK."

I'm not sure if anyone has ever found relief in hearing the words "everything will be OK" in a moment when they knew that was certainly not true. "OK" looks different for everyone, and just because the Persians say "this too shall pass" doesn't mean that it will pass "OK." So let's cut this out of our language.

I was Ms. Positive for many years. When shit really hit the fan, I had to look at the ashes of my life and wonder what to do and how to get out of it. Yet I had friends who had never seen me not positive before, and they felt the need to tell me to "just get over it," to "be positive and smile." This advice was not only not helpful but it actually held me back from healing as it fostered my anger and resentment, though I didn't know why. When I finally remembered to walk through this process, I told them to let me be as I needed to be. I told them that I needed to process it my way, they should leave if they were not able to support me through that without being fake positive and toxic. So they left.

When we are fake positive we are lying to ourselves about the impact of a situation on our life. We therefore miss the opportunity to actually make the best out of it and close ourselves off to solutions that can help us come out stronger and better on the other side. I have certainly done that before. Stuck in fake positivity, pretending that "everything will be OK," I missed proper treatment for my spine for the first week after my car accident. Well, 18 years later, it still is not "OK," but I believe I achieved the best results I could have, only because I finally looked beyond the things I wanted to see.

3| Worst-case scenario vs negative thinking

When looking at challenges and crises with my clients, I walk them through an exercise in which we discuss the worst-case scenario that could happen if everything went wrong. We talk out every angle and we make it look as dark as possible. I do this for two reasons. One, the worst-case scenario actually rarely occurs in real life, and Two, if it does, now they will be prepared for it. Then the worst-case scenario won't be *that* bad, because they will know exactly what to do and how to deal with it instead of being destroyed by surprise.

Negative thinking on the other hand doesn't serve anyone, at any time, at all. Negative thinking is when you're talking down to yourself, saying things like, "this always happens to me," and asking, "why doesn't anything good ever happen to me?" Using words like "always" or "never" can indicate negative thinking patterns when they are used to describe incidents or experiences in your life.

Entertaining negative thinking patterns is clearly not helpful and it can lead into ongoing forms of negativity, sadness, and self-defeating behavior. These patterns are subconscious and often long-practiced and we need to do our best to be aware of them, and change our language. Using the worst-case scenario technique to prepare for upcoming challenges or crises will help you see through all angles of the challenge and identify problems and their solutions that you may not be able to see when you are in the middle of the problem itself, unprepared.

4| Find a solution with what you've got, instead of making a problem out of what you don't have.

Too often, too many of us think the grass is greener on the other side of the fence. We believe that if we only had $1 million in the bank all of our problems would dissolve, and that being famous would be fun. Until we find out that's all a lie. Grass is green as is, you can't buy happiness, and most famous people don't enjoy the "being famous" part by itself, but rather the job that made them so popular.

Take what you already have and make the best out of it. Did you know there are Olympic sprinters that don't have legs? They run with prosthetic legs instead. Why do you think they can do that? Because they took what they had and found a solution, instead of creating a problem with what was missing. If you have ever traveled to a country that is less privileged or less developed than the Western countries that we know, you'd have seen kids playing outside and inventing the most creative toys. Why? Because they find solutions with what they have, instead of creating problems with what they don't have.

Having a solution-seeking mindset is absolutely crucial in factual thinking, and also for life in general. It will help you to always find a way out of any challenge, any crisis, and any situation, even when you think there is no way. If you give it enough time, look at the facts, and work with what you have, you will find it.

SECTION 4| Crisis Management

A crisis is a time of intense difficulty or danger, oftentimes in which important decisions must be made. There is a good reason why people are trained as crisis managers in different industries and why crisis management is high-priority training in the military, navy, stress and rescue teams, and any other teams who work in stressful and dangerous environments. Crisis management is a skill, and it is not an easy one to obtain. It takes years of training, role plays, practice, and tests in actual stressful environments in order for a person to be able to work in crisis.

For us as leaders, business owners, entrepreneurs, and high performers, having a minimum level of crisis management skills can be what saves our business or team by resolving stressful situations that would otherwise evolve into catastrophe.

In my time as a Team Leader for Siemens Enterprise Networks, I was quickly also made the crisis manager for the entire project. That meant talking to the CEO of Siemens Worldwide at 3 a.m. when he called me into the office to yell at me for whatever server wasn't working at that moment. In hindsight, I realized that one of the reasons I was made responsible for this role was because I wasn't emotionally attached to any of the information. IT wasn't my expertise, and I honestly couldn't care less if the new email software didn't connect, if the VPN connection wasn't working, or if a DNS server in India broke down. All I heard was "something is wrong, fix it."

Because I didn't have the depth of IT knowledge that an agent who had been working there longer would have, I didn't take any of the things the CEO said personally, and I wouldn't argue with him that any of the information he gave me was wrong. I simply took what he gave me and set out to find a solution. On the other hand, I also had nothing to lose, so when the CEO would unnecessarily swear or shout at me, I was willing to set boundaries and explain our process, which certainly didn't leave any time for cussing me out.

When it came to solving issues, my lack of IT knowledge allowed me to ask questions that were outside the box and challenged our agents to look for uncommon solutions. And sometimes it was me calling the server host in India at 2 a.m. local time to ask them to reset the server. Even though everyone was annoyed to try such a "basic" solution, they did, and 8 out of 10 times our giant problem was all resolved in just 15 easy minutes. Now, I am not promoting that not being an expert in a field helps to solve issues in times of crisis, yet a fresh set of eyes often can support the solutions that people who are in the midst of the crisis won't see.

There are three phases and ten total steps to overcoming a crisis: the Pre-Crisis Phase, which has three steps; the Crisis Phase, which has 4 steps; and the Post-Crisis Phase, which has 3 steps. Of course, there is much more to dealing with and managing crisis than can be said or learned from one section in a book, but I would like to share these steps with you because I have identified them as most important. These will help you get started with crisis management, whether that is in your life or business.

PRE-CRISIS PHASE

Whenever I train my clients on crisis management, I love to say, "The best crisis management method is crisis prevention." Because seriously, who wants a crisis in the first place? So the pre-crisis phase is the most important one to employ.

1| Plan

Plan the worst-case scenario. In the previous section, I shared how I use the worst-case scenario in order to actually be prepared for it. In order to prevent a crisis, we need to know what kind of crisis could come at us, what it might look like, and how bad it could really be. So we paint it all out, going into detail to imagine the worst case or cases indeed. And then we plan for that crisis.

Imagine you live in a place that is prone to flooding. You do not wait for a flood warning to be issued or for the water to come into your house before you save your house. You prepare yourself and your house for floods ahead of time. The same should be done in your life and in business with any crises that can be foreseen.

There are typical crisis scenarios that happen to a lot of people, yet many do not prepare for them, such as:

- A parent suddenly falls ill and has to go to the hospital

- A car accident

- An unexpected loss in the family

- Financial crisis

- Unemployment

- Family separation

...and many more. Some people believe that if you save for rainy days, then the rainy day will come, and I totally get that. If you only focus on the rainy days, they will surely show up for you often enough.

The key to crisis prevention, though, is never to look away from reality. Being blind to life and pretending nothing bad will ever happen to you will make everything that does go wrong worse, because you will not be prepared for it. It will hit you like a wrecking ball in the back of the head. And frankly, it's a little naive.

The one who is best prepared will always win, so this is what we're gonna do:

- Write out every worst-case scenario/crisis scenario that you can imagine coming up in your business. A few that come to my mind are:

- Being short on staff because many team members call out sick long-term (pandemics, flu season, any type of viruses)

- Your to-of-team expert quits and leaves behind a gap in knowledge

- Financial crisis

- Lack of customers/clients or a sudden loss of a big clientele group

- Damaging of reputation due to a scandal within the leadership team

- Sudden loss of a team member

- Come up with a plan to prevent it each scenario

- Plan how to go through each scenario, in case any of them do happen

- Set up crisis-specific roles and responsibilities

- Develop crisis-specific SOPs and workflows in order to be able to act fast, yet responsibly

- Decide what kind of language will be used during a crisis. Set up company code words, shortcuts and templates, and a set of "crisis rules" that help people act and move faster without taking things personally should communication "sound" direct rather than polite. Make clear decisions and set up rules for those decisions.

2| Test & Prove

As soon the plan has been set up, it's time to test it. This will be a staged test. The intention is for everyone to get comfortable in their crisis-management role, get familiar with following the steps and processes, and especially to stay calm and on track.

A great way to do it is for the designated crisis team to plan a day, inform clients about possible delays in responses, and share with your team that there will be crisis-training on that day. Do not tell them what the specific scenario will be. Choose one of your crisis scenarios (one that's easy to replicate without public repercussion) and recreate it as a training scenario. Involve some people from the team in the details where necessary, but the rest of the team should not know what will be happening. Then, it's go time.

The most important part is that the crisis leadership team knows their roles, guides the team through the exercise as if it were a real life experience, and also takes notes of everything along the way that did not work well or that slipped through the cracks so that later on they can be adjusted.

After the training day, the crisis team will sit together in a meeting. I prefer to do this as a workshop day, where the whole crisis training will be assessed and evaluated from different angles. How did the workflows hold up to the actual scenario? How was the understanding and reaction of the team when the crisis was called out? How was the communication between team members before, during, and after the crisis scenario? How were roles and responsibilities taken on? Have a checklist of questions that go through every step of the scenario. Let everyone share their experiences and observations. See what can be improved and optimised, and what needs further tests and adjustments, maybe with the involvement of other team members.

When tests have been successful and everything has been proven to work, finalize the crisis plans for each scenario.

3| Communicate

Communication is THE make-it-or-break-it key to crisis management. Especially in crisis prevention. It is so important. Now that you and your team have made the plan, tested it, and proved that it works, sit down with the whole team as well as with smaller circles to explain it. Explain the intention behind these plans, when to use them, as well as when not to use them, why the communication rules are the way they are, and help everyone understand how they can make the switch between a normal day to crisis scenario… and back! This will help prevent possible emotional responses and misunderstandings, and also help the team understand the exact lines and boundaries of when to use these kinds of "emergency rules" and when not to.

As mentioned above, we don't want to focus on crises and worst-case scenarios, which is why I suggest setting up this whole system in the beginning and re-visiting it once a year to keep it fresh, but in the back of your mind. It is not supposed to be an all day, every day job, because that keeps your focus on the wrong project. I absolutely believe that "where attention goes, energy flows and results show" (T. Harv Eker), and we only want to give this as much attention as is necessary.

CRISIS PHASE

We can practice and plan as much as we want, but we will never know if everything works until shit actually hits the fan. Being prepared will always trump being hit by surprise, but when crisis does strike, it can feel unexpected in the moment, even if it was not.

Since we are still in 2020 (Well, I am. You might be reading this from the future.), the global pandemic is a great example. Many people, too many people, almost all of the people who should have, did not see this coming. Why? Did they not believe a virus could travel on airplanes? Did they believe their country was immune? Are they too good to catch a virus themselves, so they don't have to care about other people? I don't know. I am throwing out random assumptions because the matter of fact is that it does not matter what they thought.

What matters is that everyone who looked past the horizon of their own plates could see this coming in some shape or form. The people who did this had a minimum of 2 or 3 months to prepare their business, their financial plan, their families, health care, travel arrangements, and everything else. I am not saying 2 or 3 months was a lot of time. But people who followed along—without a political agenda, with an open mind and curiosity for what happens in the world outside of their bubble—saw it coming. This might trigger you, and you might not like me anymore for pointing this out. Good. I think we already know I am not here to be liked. The reason why I'm telling you all this is to show you why some people are currently thriving in the 2020 disaster, while others struggle to survive.

(Disclaimer: I am talking about people who had a more-or-less functioning life and business prior to the pandemic. People who already had access to opportunities. I am not talking about people who already struggled to survive, who were fighting for their lives or dealing with other issues, many of which can be invisible.)

The steps below will show you how to navigate a crisis when it hits, whether you were prepared for it or not.

1| Breathe & Switch

This is probably the most important step, as it will decide whether or not you get through the crisis. It's your emotional response. There will be one. Handling it with care, vulnerability, and calmness will get you farther, each and every time. Can you freak out? Sure. Can you be afraid? Absolutely. Should this influence your response to the crisis? No.

Since we are talking about crisis in business here, I will stick to the COVID-19 pandemic as an example. You probably experienced it with me this year, no matter where you were in the world.

When the crisis hit and began to affect businesses, many people responded emotionally, acted out of fear, stopped their marketing completely, pivoted services, or changed their message "during this unprecedented time" because "now more than ever" would people need their help.

Others went to their rooms, felt all of the feelings, freaked out, cried, threw pillows, drank an extra glass of wine or whatever was needed—and then they paused. Before they actually acted within their business, they took emotion out of the game, not by suppressing it but by processing it.

Here's what I did, which is my favorite way to handle these kinds of things. I call it the "7-minute breakdown." When I feel overwhelmed and extremely stressed in times of crisis, I can feel the peak coming. I take time off for this exercise and lock myself in my house. I get enough water, tissues, and pen and paper ready.

I set a timer for 7 minutes, look at the situation, and let all of the bottled-up emotions roll over me. I sit in them, I cry, scream, I curse the fuck out of it, I complain, I cry more, and most importantly, I rant and whine about it as much as I must—for 7 minutes. When the alarm goes off, I stop. Yes, just like that. Then I laugh, watch a funny video, dance to one of my happy songs, and get back on track. For some of us, that may not be enough time to process all of the emotions and feelings that come up, and that's fine. What it does is to help give you some relief and a clear head for what's to come. I use the pen and paper to write down all of the complaints, whinings, rants, and self-defeating thoughts. At the end of the 7 minute mark, I go outside and burn it.

That may sound really dramatic, and it is. I laugh every time I tell my clients to do it, and they think it is quite over-the-top. Until they do it. They then send me funny GIFs and admit how much of a relief it is. It is! Unreleased emotions and feelings can get stuck in our bodies and minds. That's one way I get migraines.

After you have gone through the "7-minute breakdown," take some deep breaths. Let it be 3 or 5 breaths, or five whole minutes. Sit still and do it. Then switch into crisis mode by activating your clear thoughts with a rational approach to finding solutions.

2| The bigger picture

After you take some deep breaths and make the switch, take a step back and look at the bigger picture. Can you see a pattern? Can you see the root of the crisis? Is the solution coming up somewhere between the lines? Can you think outside the box?

Looking at the bigger picture needs time, space, and the permission to step away. In a crisis, that's the hardest part to do. Most of us just want to jump right in and solve the problem, stop the crisis, and turn the situation around. But when you do not stop and look at the bigger picture first, you will miss important things.

This does not need weeks, days, or even hours of your time. Start with one. Take one hour of your time to lock yourself away with just a pen, a bunch of paper, and maybe some necessary information printed out. No phone. No laptop. No one around for that hour.

For the first 15 minutes, I highly recommend taking some deep breaths. Let all the thoughts about the crisis scenario come in. Let them all rush over you like an avalanche. And write them down. Each single one of them, no matter how embarrassing, shameful, weird, self-defeating, or nonsensical they may be. Write them all down.

Now look at these thoughts. Which ones are just baseless thoughts? Meaning, which ones are not factual? A great process to go through is Byron Katie's method of self-inquiry called "the work," found in her book *The Four Questions*. If you'd like to find out more about it and learn the process, check out the book experience at www.thetimemethod.com/

bookexperience. We will link to her work and resources you can sign up for.

Strike out the thoughts on this piece of paper that are neither true (e.g. "I never get things right;" "This is all my fault") nor helpful will help you create a more open and clear headspace for the 45 minutes ahead.

For the next 30 minutes, take a second piece of paper and start writing down all of the facts about the situation. What happened? How did it start? Is someone responsible for it? If so, why? What are possible next steps or even next consequences? Can things get worse? If so, how?

Now look at the helpful thoughts that you wrote down on your first sheet of paper and see how they correlate. Is there a solution showing up? Is there a root cause you can look at? Can you see a gap?

For the last 15 minutes, take another piece of paper and write all possible solutions out, whether they seem feasible, logical, and reasonable or you dream up a random, magical, fairy-dust solution. Write it all out.

3| What are you not seeing?

So many of us think that, as a leader, we need to do the hard work alone. We think we can't ask for support or invite our team to the solution-finding process. I'll tell you right now: you are missing out. I am 100% sure that 5 people have many better ideas than one person does. It's a numbers game. So let's play.

Invite the team to your "big picture session" after you finish your hour by yourself. You can choose to only invite your leadership team, or you can invite the senior levels with them, or you can ask everyone to join.

Avoid setting the team up with a bias by sharing only the facts of the situation at first. Explain your intention, for the team to find the best possible solution to the crisis. Don't share your thoughts, and don't share anything that could be distracting to the team or push them in a certain direction. The situation should basically be explained in one sentence.

Then ask the whole team, "What am I not seeing?"

Give them 5 minutes after you've shared the facts to write down their thoughts, their views and possible solutions. Let them know that no thought and no solution is too absurd or abstruse. After the 5 minutes are up, let everyone share their thoughts and ideas as well as the way they see the situation and a possible way out. You can choose to let everyone speak as long as they wish, or set a timer of 2 to 5 minutes, depending on how big your team is. For smaller teams you can give each person 10 minutes to speak. When everyone has spoken, it is time for you to share your own thoughts and the solution process that you previously came up with. Give the team 30 minutes to discuss all possible solutions, dismissing the ones that are great ideas but not reasonable, feasible, or possible to act on right now.

The goal is to have an action plan by the end of the meeting. That meeting can be as short as 1 hour if guided properly, or as long as 3 to 4 hours with bigger teams. However long it takes, the outcome will be a solution that will probably save you time, money, and nerves. You'll also gain a lot of trust, loyalty, and likeability from your team when you do this right.

4| Act

Now that you and your team have found a great solution, and possibly a backup plan, it's time to act! Maybe you have no real solution at all, but you do have a plan for tackling the next few weeks and how you will take care of your customers and clients. Even in crisis, never forget about the people outside of your business who have supported you and who pay for your products and services.

When acting in times of crisis, it is critical to stay calm, keep a factual-thinking mindset, take on only high-priority tasks, and trust that everyone else knows their jobs and will do them well. This is certainly no time for nit-picking, and it's no time for control freaks or micromanagers to come out waving their hands everywhere.

The way we communicate with our team, peers, customers, and partners in times of crisis is extremely important. I always recommend transparency, which does not necessarily mean that everyone needs to know everything. Some companies are transparent in that literal fashion and it works great for them. But what I mean when I recommend transparency is that everyone knows what they need to know and is able to access all knowledge and information regarding themselves, their position, and their environment. That means that if one or two people are responsible for the crisis in some way, they should know that immediately and they should be informed about how that will be handled as soon the crisis has been solved. If there are steps that must be taken immediately, like putting someone on temporary leave in order to prevent further damage, that must be communicated with the team member along with the process they should expect. The reason for the decision should be shared with them as well as with the whole team. Transparency in that circumstance helps stop people from spreading stories that may or may not be true or gossiping in a way that does not align with company values (which is behavior that in itself should be looked into, in my eyes).

Transparency with customers and clients looks a little different, but looking at 2020 and the pandemic as an example again, a LOT of companies had issues with delivery, production, sourcing ingredients, and so on, but they did not inform their customers about it. At least not until the issue was so obvious that customers informed themselves about it and made the public story about the situation a whole lot worse than the company's press release could have been.

Being honest and transparent with our customers and clients is such a big opportunity. It shows that you take responsibility, not only as a business but as the CEO and a human yourself. Everyone can relate to being a human. We all have to battle with crises here and there. We all have to overcome challenges, but hiding from them never made anyone a hero.

Being transparent about a situation, about steps being taken and about possible consequences or changes, can help to build trust and likeability with existing customers and clients as well as with new ones who are watching what your business and your industry peers are doing in these times. If you do it right, business may very well pick up because of how you handled this crisis together with your team.

POST-CRISIS PHASE

The crisis is over, but it's not time to relax quite yet. There is a final, very crucial step we can't miss, and that's the evaluation!

We have to look back at the scenario and walk through a few more things before we can take a break.

But first things first, take a step back. Breathe. Look around and let it all sink in. It's okay to let a few days pass in order to fathom everything that happened, what the crisis was about, how it worked out, what happened, what consequences arose, and so on.

When you are ready for it, plan a day or two to go through the following steps together with your team.

1| Evaluate

Evaluating and assessing the crisis, from the time it erupted up until the moment you sit down to do the evaluation, is the most important part of moving forward and onward from the crisis. Each of the steps from the pre-crisis phase and the crisis phase should be looked at and walked through. This is best done with the dedicated crisis management team.

Since this is a rather long task, I suggest booking a 2 to 3 day time slot and preparing this in a workshop setting. At the beginning of the meeting, let everyone write out their impressions, thoughts, and evaluation of each of the phases in general, from pre-crisis buildup through post-crisis cooldown. Are there any special remarks? Did anyone stand out to you during this time? If so, how? How did the team work together? How were crisis workflows, communication, and other specific sets of rules followed? Did they work? These are just a few questions that everyone can think about.

When thoughts have been written out, start with Phase 1: Pre-Crisis. Let everyone share an overview of their thoughts on it and then dive deep into each step of the phase. The following questions will help with the review of each step, you can add other questions or replace some depending on your situation.

- How was this step set up/prepared?

- What are lessons learned during the preparation and execution of this step?

- What worked very well?

- What can / must be improved?

- Who should be responsible for this step and its adjustment?

Go through both Pre-Crisis and Crisis Phase and evaluate each of the 7 steps. By the end of the evaluation, you will have deep insight of the sequence of the crisis from the different perspectives of your crisis team members and yourself.

The next step is to take all of the information you have and go back to the drawing board. Go back to step one, phase one: planning for the crisis. The difference this time is that now you are not planning a new version but optimizing, adjusting, and changing or cutting what doesn't fit. These adjustments will definitely be at least another day's worth of work or, if loads of improvements are necessary, it might take two days. If it is a lot to work on, consider splitting the crisis team members into different groups to be more efficient and also to have the team focus on their specialties.

On the third day, walk through the results together with the team, discuss different strategies or possibilities of implementing the changes, and have an action plan ready to go.

Don't forget to celebrate coming out on the other side of a crisis. No matter what.

2| Adapt

The crisis plan is optimized, the implementation strategy is ready to go. Now it is time to adopt and integrate the changes you've decided on. Send the crisis team members out to communicate, implement, test, and prove the new crisis plan. Maybe some people need to be trained or retrained, maybe new codes are needed. Let them get feedback for everything and be sure to be their number one supporter along the way.

It matters how this implementation is delivered. Make sure the team knows how they have done and how and where they can improve, but also be sure to celebrate them and thank them for their hard work during this time. Being recognized and feeling appreciated is what makes team members perform at higher levels for you.

This step may be the shortest of them all, but it is almost certainly the one that will take the longest to get right.

3| Inspire

Lastly, it is just as important to take feedback for yourself on board. You can send out an anonymous survey asking for feedback about how you handled the crisis, or you can ask people yourself. You can also include the request in the evaluation workshop. No matter how you ask for your feedback, make sure what you receive is plentiful and truthful. The goal is to improve, not to hear something nice about yourself (unless that's absolutely the only truth!). If there are things to improve, which usually is the case, make it a point to find them and adjust what didn't work well.

Use this feedback to improve your own growth, and also to inspire your team. You'll remind them to always have integrity, to stay true to your values, and to put growth over convenience.

You'll inspire them to always be the best version of yourself. And who wouldn't want to work for and with someone who inspires them like that?

What a lot of people get wrong when they manage or lead teams is that they try to influence how their team members take action. Neil Strauss said it best. "Shaming someone into action creates acting. Inspiring someone into action creates change."

Then the question to ask yourself is, "Do you want your team to act, or to facilitate change?"

CRISIS MANAGEMENT

 www.moniquelindner.com

 @themoniquelindner

# CHAPTER REVIEW

By now we know that developing and improving our mindset is a lifetime's work. But it shouldn't be 'hard' or feel like torture. To help you get into the work of this chapter a little more with ease I have a few questions for you that I'd love for you to ponder upon and answer for yourself.

You can use them as journal prompts, meditate on them or discuss them with friends or whomever you feel safe with to share these:

1. What does discipline mean to you in your daily life? What does it look like? What does it not look like?

2. Where are you currently not taking responsibility for your life or business?

3. How many hard conversations do you have daily? With whom?

4. How comfortable are you to show emotions in different types of situations?

5. Does vulnerability make you feel uncomfortable? If yes, why? If no, why not?

6. In what areas of your life would factual thinking be currently beneficial to you?

7. Are you prepared for a crisis? How does it look like for you to be prepared? Why or why not would you prepare for a crisis in your life/business?

Energy Efficiency

My clinical death was the biggest blessing of my life. My migraines are my greatest teacher and my best friend.

If it wasn't for my clinical death I wouldn't have gotten even a glimpse of the strength that's inside of me. I thought that 15 years of extreme physical pain and emotional suffering had taught me what "being strong" meant, but a cardiac arrest took this to another dimension completely. I still don't recommend anyone try dying and coming back just for the fun of it. But I cannot deny what the experience, and the process of unfolding that it kicked off, has done for me.

Without this cardiac arrest, I would have never doubted the way I was living so early in my life, which means that I wouldn't have been able to change it completely within the next 7 years, all while building a great career along the way. I also would have never doubted the credibility of the medical industry, as I do, were it not for witnessing an entire onsite ER team fail to recognize my own cardiac arrest. I wouldn't have scrutinized all of the medication that I was blindly taking, given to me by doctors that were happily welcoming me back into their offices each month. I probably wouldn't have started traveling solo just 6 months later. Before my clinical death, I would have let fear of (insert anything that can happen when you travel solo) talk me out of it.

But I just wasn't afraid anymore, I guess. Or maybe the fear of dying, this time for real, without having done all of the things I always wanted to do, was driving me forward.

Years ago I lived in crippling fear of what would come up next on my "disease to overcome" list. For all of these years I was my mum's "sick little girl," and it was disturbing, to say the least. Especially because, ironically, I never *felt* sick. I didn't feel like anyone needed to treat me special. I didn't feel like I needed to use my diseases as an excuse. I hated it when my family members treated me like I was dumb or unable to achieve anything, told me I was "nothing but ill," a burden. So I became a high achiever.

Achieving has been my greatest coping mechanism, and it turned into one of my biggest strengths. Many people couldn't deal with or keep up with this. It's interesting how people see you as a "sick, weak girl," underestimating you while you smile and wave—until you surpass them and achieve more than they could ever imagine in their wildest dreams. At this point, I am still smiling and waving. Just without the fake friends on the sidelines.

My migraines, though, are my best friend. Sounds weird, yeah? Yeah. See, they've never lied to me. Ever. Not when I was 4 and they first started, trying to show me all of the dangerous and unhealthy things going on around me. Not when I was 15 and the epileptic seizures became so strong they regularly knocked me unconscious and sent me to the hospital, trying to show me that there was something really wrong in my life. They also didn't lie to me when I was 19 and they killed me. Every single seizure, migraine attack, and later on, my occipital neuralgia showed me that something was wrong. They gave me a sign. Often enough, they were saving me from something worse: abuse.

I have checked quite a few boxes of abuse in my life, from mental and emotional to physical and sexual abuse. I have always been a trigger for people. My energy and the strength I carry simply is so powerful that people are either drawn to me, repelled by me, or triggered by me. The ones who were triggered are usually the ones who hurt me the worst. My existence triggered all of their insecurities, shadows, and fears. But no one ever was and no one ever will be able to break me or tear me down. That might be the biggest trigger for many people. They can feel that no matter what they do, they simply can't bring me down. And that is the power of energy.

I suppressed all this throughout most of my childhood, teenage, and young adult years. I tried hard to fit in, belong somewhere, and be more likeable… which obviously didn't work. Not only did people like me less when they finally got to know me better, they would either be unreliable when I needed their support or they would eventually leave me when they realised the impact my illnesses had on my life.

I had a friend for 12 years whose life was completely opposite my own. She was from a small countryside town and although she surely had her own problems throughout her childhood and experienced typical daily-life issues, there wasn't anything that really challenged her. She had never experienced trauma, sudden loss, or extreme grief, and she was visibly irritated when I talked about my experiences. Ironically, we became friends because she was the only one that helped me in college when I had a migraine attack with seizures in school. I fell semi-dramatically from my chair as I went unconscious, hitting my head hard on the floor as I dropped from the seizure. She helped me and waited for my dad and the emergency responders while everyone else left the classroom.

We spent years and years together from then on, and some years we even spent everyday together. But something was off. See, I didn't take time off when I had migraines because that wasn't an option for me then. I'd still be around people, I'd still be out, I'd still go to work—I lived a rather "normal" life, just with an "add-on" that happened to be excruciating pain, speech impairment, spatial perception impairment, and other dysfunctions of the brain including periodic seizures. But I never stayed home. I chose to live instead of just exist. I never complained. I would mention when I wasn't okay, or when I needed to go home, or when I needed someone to get me water. And yes, I definitely made my life more difficult than it could have been, but I also just didn't see how I could miss out on life 5 times a week for more than 2 decades, so I trained myself to be able to participate, just like everyone else. Some time into our friendship she started to complain about me. "You are always sick." "You always have something dramatic going on in your life." "Can you not just be normal?" Ha. Yeah, great question.

No. I can not. Thanks for asking.

Normal is not what I am striving for. Normal sounds like a really average and undesirable thing to me. Normal literally sounds like death. Existing instead of living. Things happening to you instead of for you. Life in other people's hands instead of yours.

Normal sounds like a punishment. So no, I can not and will not be normal.

But somehow, maybe because I wanted a friend, I tried. I tried that normal thing. I didn't talk about my pain or my abuse. And that's where it all went wrong. See, this all started way earlier than this particular friend. The pressure to be more "normal" started when I was 5. But this story is so typical of how things always happened, how we are made to fit into the mold, how we are told to be more "normal"… like, what the fuck does "normal" even mean?

All this molding, brainwashing, and normalizing took a huge toll on my energy. That bold, powerful aura that comes from deep within. Everyone is born with it. We are all born with some kind of energy, unique like a fingerprint. We carry it deep inside, and it shines through us. It builds an aura around us, just like a halo around the moon. You can not get rid of it, it is always there. You can, like I did, suppress it, hide it, try to swallow it or mask it. But you can not get rid of it. When you do not align with your energy, everything else will be out of whack, too. Your body, mind, and spirit. They will fight your oppression. They are not here to conform.

I say "align" instead of "balance" because I don't believe in balance in life. There is duality, and there is equalizing energies, but there is no balance in the sense of a scale that's on a perfect horizontal stand.

I needed to tell you these stories because I know I am not alone. I know we all go through periods of suppressing who we really are and having others trying to force us into a box that fits society's expectations. But we are who we are. And living life trying to be someone else just to fit the mold is a fucking waste of time.

When we come into this world with our energy, we are not told how to preserve it and use it, or how to prevent others from abusing it or sucking it from us. We are simply not efficient with it. That's what this chapter is all about. For the next few sections of the book, I will go deeper into a few of the steps that I took to break out of the mold, create my own self, and most importantly, to preserve and step into my full energy.

Sounds woo? Good. You'll get into it soon. It's not that witchy, I promise.

SECTION 1| Detox: People, Activities, & Materialistic Things

The reason I told you the story of my "friend" is because she was one of the biggest lessons for me in regards to detoxing my life.

Up to this point I thought I was really good at choosing my friends. Weren't they always there when I needed them? Weren't they rooting for me and my success? Weren't they happy for me when I was happy and supported me when I needed help?

This is indeed what it looked like from the outside. But when I looked deeper, I recalled many situations where I had to admit I had let them off the hook with a lot of bullshit. With a lot of gaslighting, fearmongering, brainwashing, and manipulation techniques that I wasn't aware of then. I am very sure that much of it was unconscious. It was their bias speaking, things they had been taught from early childhood as well as their insecurities that spoke for them.

That excuse doesn't make it any better or less painful, however. In the past two decades I have been blessed to learn how to detox. That process is about detoxing more than people, but detoxing people is certainly the hardest part. In this section, I will share my knowledge about how to detox so that you can stay in your full energy, be yourself, and live your life unapologetically.

1| DETOX PEOPLE THAT DON'T SERVE YOUR ENERGY ANYMORE

We meet a lot of people in life and not all of them can be aligned with us. As we evolve and grow, our energy and vibration changes, unfolds, and rises.

In my late teens and early twenties, my energy must have been on a rather low frequency. I had been through so much but wasn't yet processing any of it properly. That certainly attracted people with the same vibration. Don't worry, I am not going to preach the law of attraction or anything like it, even if you think it sounds like it. I am not a fan of LOA but I do know that there are certain laws of physics and metaphysical concepts that relate to the human experience.

For a better understanding of what detoxing means in the context of detoxing from other people, let's have a look at the dictionary. The Oxford Dictionary says that to "detox" means to "abstain from or rid the body of toxic or unhealthy substances." In this context, we are talking about distancing ourselves in space and time from people who are not supporting our growth anymore, who are engaging behaviors that are toxic for us, who are draining our energy, and whose presence in our life no longer serves us. Oftentimes this means that it's time to go separate ways. We need to choose a new path that does not include them.

What toxic behavior means is subjective. What is toxic to me is not necessarily toxic to you. Toxic behavior exists on a spectrum. Some people may just be annoying, frustrating, difficult, demanding, or generally unpleasant to be around. If that's the case, it is good to stay at a comfortable distance, but these people are most likely not engaging in toxic behavior. And just as there is a range of toxic behavior from others, there is a range of tolerance to it on our side. You may give more leeway to your brother than you would to your colleague. We all have different thresholds, and it's important to discover yours.

When we talk about toxic people, we are talking about the people who infiltrate our lives, affect our daily wellbeing, and oftentimes our mental health. At work or in business, this can have a huge effect on your performance. Unfortunately, the people closest to us are the ones who can have the biggest negative impact on us.

Let's go through a list of questions to help you see whether you need to go through a detox process from someone in your life.

1| What are the warning signs and red flags?

It can be hard to see the truth, especially when it involves the people closest to you that you love and respect. But if they have a negative effect on your life, the most loving thing you can do is distance yourself. There are quite a few signs of toxicity to look for. Here are a few:

- *Toxic people want to take control of you*

Toxic people oftentimes do not have control over their own lives. Instead, they seek ways to control other things, like other people and other people's lives, in order to feel more powerful and less insecure. They can do this with blatantly controlling methods or with more subtle techniques.

- *Toxic people disrespect your boundaries*

Boundaries are very important in interpersonal relationships. When we set boundaries we do so for the benefit of both sides. Boundaries outline what behaviors are safe, clear, and permissible and help everyone understand expectations. Toxic people will straight up disregard and disrespect your boundaries, pushing on them until they cross them. They will sometimes judge you for boundaries, or use them against you to explain why you are the "bad" person. Violating boundaries is a toxic person's favorite red flag.

- *Toxic people use manipulation tactics to get what they want/ need from you*

Ugh. This one is a hard pill to swallow. It sounds malicious but I have found that many of the people who do this are not aware of their toxic behavior. They manipulate you because that is all they know, or it is the only way they have ever received love or attention or validation. They have been conditioned to use manipulation. Others manipulate with intention, and those are the people who are most dangerous because they know exactly how to manipulate you. While the former group of people may be open to feedback, you will likely hit a wall of resistance because they are unaware of their behavior. In both cases, you need to cut ties.

- *Toxic people use gaslighting to make you feel inferior, and doubt yourself in any way*

Gaslighting is a 2020 trigger word, but it has its place. Wikipedia describes gaslighting as "a form of psychological manipulation in which a person or a group covertly sows seeds of doubt in a targeted individual or group, making them question their own memory, perception, or judgment, often evoking in them cognitive dissonance and other changes including low self-esteem." Having experienced a life-time of gaslighting, in many shapes and forms by many different people who used it consciously and unconsciously, I can confirm that the outcome, once the seed is sowed, is disturbing.

People who gaslight use denial, misdirection, misinformation, and contradiction to destabilize the victim or the receiver. A typical example is to belittle and invalidate someone by denying that their experiences ever happened, or insisting that the victim is "making it up in their mind" (one of my absolute "favorites"). For me, the damage lasted in a lack of trust in myself and my intuition (which got me into further trouble). I doubted myself constantly and experienced self hatred, extreme low self-esteem, and no self confidence. The amount of work I have since done to unlearn, relearn, and undo the damage of long-term gaslighting is phenomenal—if there was an award for it, I'd take it.

- *Toxic people don't take self-responsibility*

If anyone around you or close to you is blaming and shaming anything and everyone else for their circumstances, run! There will always be circumstances outside of our control that influence the outcomes of our work, effort, and our results. Yet, by taking self-responsibility, we are able to take our power back and make the best out of any situation. This does not mean we can prevent these situations, but we can influence the impact they have on our lives. If a person is looking to blame all of their mistakes, failures, and miserable situations on outside circumstances, or if they are trying to find reasons to manipulate you by judging you instead of actually looking inward at themselves, then it's time to run. People who constantly blame and shame others for their own mistakes and wrongdoings simply will not take self-responsibility for anything.

- *Toxic people are not honest*

I am not talking about storytelling exaggeration here and there, or giving someone face-saving "yes, it's that way" directions when you don't actually know where the address is. I am talking about someone who straight-out lies to your face and uses a pattern of dishonesty for their own benefit. Toxic people also use dishonesty to separate people into opposing groups, pitting them against each other for the benefit of the toxic person.

There are many more examples of red flags for toxic behavior, but these are the most common and the ones that are most damaging to our own behavior, thinking, and emotional wellbeing. If you see any of these signs in a person close to you, it is time to make a decision.

2| How do you know if you need to detox from people in your life?

It's time to consider a detox when any of the above behaviors have showed up in your relationship with a friend, partner, family member, colleague, or someone else in your life, and you have already tried the following steps:

- Bring awareness to the situation

- Let the other person know that the behavior/situation makes you uncomfortable

- Ask for their thoughts and talk about ways it can be solved

- Have an open and honest conversation about your needs and boundaries

- Be open to hearing their perspective and ask if there is anything you can improve

- Improve, if it feels reasonable and is something you want to commit to

- Check progress on both sides

To implement these steps I highly recommend using a communication framework such as the nonviolent communication approach described by Marshall Rosenberg.

If any and/or all of these steps have been implemented and nothing has changed, it is time to reflect on how this relationship affects you. Answer the following questions with yes or no.

1. Do you feel exhausted, drained, and sapped of your energy after meeting or calling that person?

   YES / NO

2. Is this person always the center of attention? Even when it is you who needs help or support, do they make it about themselves?

   YES / NO

3. Are they hanging from your big dreams like a rock, bringing you "down to earth" and just "keeping it real" instead of dreaming big with you and having your back?

   YES / NO

4. Do they cling to drama and negativity like a magnet, always insisting that any suggestion or piece of advice for help and improvement will not work for them?

YES / NO

5. Do they judge every step you take, every decision you make, and all of your opinions, always offering unsolicited "advice" for how you could be doing better?

YES / NO

6. Do you start doubting yourself or sinking into misery, irritability, and low self-esteem whenever you spend time with this person?

YES / NO

7. Are you avoiding this person, replying late to messages and not answering spontaneous calls?

YES / NO

8. Are you engaging in more negative thinking after a meeting or call with this person than you did before seeing/speaking to them?

YES / NO

9. Do they take you on "emotional rollercoasters" sometimes, no matter in which direction?

YES / NO

10. Are they taking much more than they are giving in your relationship?

YES / NO

Any question answered with YES is an indication to look deeper into the issue. More than 3 questions answered with YES should be an alarm for you to pack up and leave. But it is often not that easy to just go.

3| How to cut ties with a toxic person?

If all conversations about the issue so far have been ignored or led to no solution, then it is time to set strong and firm boundaries and stick with them. In the next section we talk more extensively about setting boundaries, so I will leave it at that for now. It is also time for you to make a decision about how to continue on with this person, or if you even want to continue on at all. A lot of people leave the decision-making to the toxic person because they don't want to be seen as rude, oversensitive, unreasonable, or an asshole, but you are being all of these things to yourself when you do not cut ties with toxic people.

Making a decision about what is right for you (which can be different from what you *feel* would be good for you) and acting on that decision will help you preserve energy and take the power back into your own hands. Making decisions about people with toxic behavior can be painful, because we often doubt ourselves, our judgement, and our ability to make the right choice. That's what toxicity does. It infiltrates your system and gets you to doubt yourself to the core, even about the simplest things.

Once you have set boundaries and made a decision about how to go ahead or not to do so, you need to communicate your decision. While text messages are surely a convenient way, I recommend communicating the boundaries and decisions in person or by phone in order to express the urgency of the message. If this will drain you of too much energy, or if you feel like the risk of being manipulated out of your decision is too high, then it is totally okay to write up a kind but firm statement and send it by message or email or any other digital form.

This process is often messy and painful. All of the self-doubt and negative and derogatory thoughts you have about yourself will come back, especially during the decision-making process and in the moment you deliver the message. Stick through it. This is not your voice. Stick with your decision and walk away with your head high. For the sake of your sanity, stick to your own core values. That means that even though you will wish you could scream and yell at them, curse them out or call them names, don't. Well, unless those are some of your core values. But I believe people who read this book mostly hold very high-vibe core values. Stick to them. They will guide you through this process and help you to work through the residual damage this toxic experience has left in your life.

If a toxic person has been drawing massive benefits from their relationship with you, they may not let you go "just like that." They may open their trick box and use all of the manipulation techniques, gaslighting methods, lies, and everything else inside to keep you in their reins. In my opinion, your best bet here is to say "yes, you are absolutely right" to *whatever* they say, and then run, or block them in any form, from their phone number and social media to real life encounters.I found that putting my ego aside, telling them they are right and walking away, had a silencing effect on many toxic people. You validated them, agreed with their words that that you are a bad/stupid/useless/unworthy person, yet you walked away. With your words you affirmed them, yet with your actions you showed them that they are wrong. This does not work with every type of toxic person, but it works with many. When in doubt, block.

4| What happens after I successfully cut ties with a toxic person?

After cutting ties and leaving a toxic relationship behind, it's time to enter phase II of the hard work: recovery and rebuilding.

Every person that comes into our life and stays for a while leaves an influence that affects us. People engaging in toxic behavior have a negative influence. As described above, some common lingering effects of being around toxic people for a long time can include self-doubt, low self-esteem, decreased self-confidence, not trusting your intuition or instincts anymore, not trusting yourself and your decisions anymore, second-guessing every step you make, negative thinking, doubting your sanity, and other effects along the same lines.

If you experience any of these after a period of interacting with a toxic person the best thing I can recommend is finding support. It can be a friend, a therapist, a coach, a support group, or even a book that can help you to understand these patterns and work through them. I have benefitted from many of these different options alongside traditional Chinese medicine, energy work, reiki, and other healing modalities.

During my recovery and rebuilding process, it was essential for me to be patient and kind with myself. I took the time to understand the patterns and how to recognise and break them (because they will probably return in the future in some way or another), and learn to make healthy decisions earlier. How long this work will take is up to you.

5| What about toxic activities and materialistic things?

If this section is about detoxing from people, activities, and materialistic things, why have I only talked about people so far? I'm glad you asked. That's because detoxing from people is the hardest part of the work.

The only hard part about cutting toxic activities and materialistic things out of our lives is the emotional attachment we hold to these things. A lot of times we are using them as coping mechanisms, as a means of validation, or as a filler for a void. But activities and things can't give us any of these. We have to give them to ourselves first.

So let's look into some examples. These are listed without any judgement, simply based on the fact that these activities or materialistic things are harmful to our system, and can even be harmful to other people:

- Smoking, drinking alcohol, and taking drugs including abusing pharmaceuticals

- Excessive partying that includes severe sleep deprivation for an extended time

- Eating junk food way too often

- Racing your car or motorcycle in normal, day-to-day traffic instead of on racetracks

- Hunting wild animals just for the trophy (e.g. elephants)

- Obsessively buying luxury goods that you don't need or have a use for (e.g. expensive cars, watches, bags, etc.) to make yourself "happy"

This could be a much longer list, or shorter, depending on your beliefs. But this is not just about morals, it is about the intention behind the actions.

If you are a millionaire who is happy with or without money and it just so happens that you did work hard and became wealthy and now one of your joys is to buy and restore oldtimer cars, then yay! Go you! There's absolutely nothing wrong with this. If you are a millionaire who feels empty inside and you don't have much to live for, and you buy a garage full of lamborghinis and ferraris and film vlogs for your youtube channel to gain more status and fake friends, this is a form of toxic behavior to look in to.

6| How do I identify what is toxic for me and what not?

Everyone is different and that's a good thing. That also means what is toxic for me doesn't have to be toxic for you. Just as there are red flags for toxic people, there are also indicators for toxic activities and materialistic things:

- *Buying things for the purpose of filling a void, increasing your status, gaining (fake) friends, or making yourself (fake) happy* will leave you emptier than you were before you bought that thing. Once the adrenalin rush of having bought this new piece is over, you may experience sadness, anger, or frustration for spending a lot of money without getting what you actually wanted. This feeling may not be front and center at first, but it can creep in like a whisper and slowly develop into a nagging voice in the back of your mind.

- *Engaging in certain activities leaves you feel low on energy,* or exhausted/dirty/ashamed/guilty/empty/frustrated with yourself and it takes a while to recover.

- *You only engage in some activities because of peer pressure,* but you don't actually want to take part. They don't make you feel good and you experience self-loathing and negative thinking afterwards.

- *You buy certain goods because "everyone has to have them,"* but you actually don't really care about having these items and you resent yourself for spending so much money on them.

- *You are using certain substances for the sake of reducing stress,* anxiety, or other symptoms, but you wish you didn't need them

Certainly there are many more scenarios that fall into this category, but these are quite common ones that we can find in our daily lives. You may feel resistance when first considering these activities. You may think that you have a good reason for doing any one of these things and not want to stop doing it, and that's absolutely fine.

If your goal is to increase, preserve, and be more efficient with your energy levels, then it is worth a look into the activity. Follow the resistance. Ask yourself what the benefits you gain from these activities or purchases are, and what the disadvantages are. When we explore our behavior this way, we sometimes find that the only benefit is that we can keep hiding from addressing the root cause of our symptoms. This is a painful yet worthy path to walk.

To identify red flags before you engage in these activities or buy new things you may not even need or want, you can ask yourself the following questions:

- What are my intentions for engaging in this activity or buying this thing?

    - Is it for the sole purpose of bringing me true joy?

    - Am I trying to make myself happy, fill a void, or increase my status?

- How does engaging in the activity make me feel once it is over?

    - I feel the same as before, content with myself.

    - I feel low on energy, sad or depressed, exhausted, or even guilty and ashamed for engaging in it, or it takes days for me to recover.

- How does buying that thing make you feel like once you've had it for a while?

    - It still brings me joy when I see it, and I like to engage with it regularly, but it doesn't change my state of contentment.

    - I went back to the same state I was in before I bought it, and now I feel like I need something new or I even forgot I bought it.

The only caveat here is that you have to be 100% honest with yourself. This can be an issue if we are stuck knee-deep in these behaviors.

To be 100% honest with yourself means that we need to be self-aware, not in hindsight but in the present moment. That can only be achieved through extensive practice and repetition. My best suggestion for this work is again to look for and reach out to support.

SECTION 2| Boundaries, Standards, & Expectations

I have mentioned setting boundaries quite a few times throughout the book so far, and it's about time we really talk about it. But why did I choose to discuss it here, in the chapter about energy efficiency, and not in a chapter about leadership or any of the other pillars? Quite simply, it's because if you are able to set firm boundaries, have quality (and yes, high) standards, and you are able to manage your own and other people's expectations well, then you get two results from it: 1) high energy levels and 2) everything else after energy levels will fall into place in regards to the other pillars.

Before we get started, let's look at some definitions and the differences between these three descriptors.

Boundaries, also known as personal boundaries in the context we are talking about, are a set of rules, limitations, and guidelines that we create in order to safely and reasonably interact with other people and identify permissible ways for others to behave towards us. Setting boundaries also entails consequences should our rules not be followed, and includes an understanding of the ways we will react in case our limits are pushed or crossed.

For example: "If we meet for the first time, you can not hug me."

Standards are personal norms or requirements that we establish to indicate the level of quality at which we will perform, and the quality level that we expect others to match or exceed. These standards can be set in our personal life as well as our business. The idea of setting standards is common in many industries when handling standard operating procedures.

For example: "If we are friends, I will check in with you at least once a week."

The difference between a personal boundary and a standard is that a boundary is a limit that we want other people to not cross, while a standard is what we want people to deliver. In short, a boundary says, "No. Not any further," and a standard says, "Yes, this is the minimum I want to see."

Expectations are strong beliefs or assumptions about upcoming events, behaviors, or situations. Expectations are always biased, since they are based on our own knowledge, experiences, and memories as well as emotions such as fear.

For example: "I expect the weather to be cold and rainy in December in Germany."

Expectations can be helpful or harmful. It depends how we use them and how we take ownership of them. We also must realize that we don't know another person's expectations until we ask them.

When we are able to set firm boundaries and high standards, then we should be able to manage our expectations properly as well, and there should be no surprises. We will discuss this further in the following sections of this chapter.

1| IDENTIFYING & SETTING BOUNDARIES

In my experience, identifying and setting boundaries is the hardest part of these 3 descriptors. Over the past six years I have had to learn over and over again how to identify my own boundaries in different settings and situations, with different people, and also for myself and my own lifestyle. It's an ongoing process to learn all of them. The most helpful resource that I have found in the past year was the course on boundaries by Mark Groves.

I have learned one big fact in all these years: We do not set boundaries as children, and in fact, we don't see many boundaries set around us at all. The ones that do are blessed to grow up with such healthy knowledge. I am no expert on the topic but I do know how important it is, especially in terms of managing your energy. I am going to share what I have learnt so far with you. If you want to dive deeper, I highly recommend checking out some of the resources I have put together to share with you in the digital book experience at www.thetimemethod.com/bookexperience.

How to identify boundaries or the lack thereof?

Here are a set of questions to help you to explore your relationship to boundaries and discover where you may want to set a stricter version of boundaries for yourself.

- Did you experience boundaries as a child? How? From whom did you experience them?

- How were boundaries used in your childhood? In a healthy form? As punishment?

- Did other people set boundaries with you, but you were not allowed to have any?

- Did/Do people often push back on your boundaries when you attempt to set them or make them clear?

- Do you have trouble sticking to your own boundaries? If so, why?

- Do you feel stressed, exhausted, frustrated, anxious, depressed, or even mad after interactions with certain people?

- Do certain phrases, movements, actions, or anything else trigger a sudden, intense emotional reaction in you?

- Are there any actions or behaviors you wish other people would stop directing at you?

- Are you being pulled into certain conversations that you are not comfortable with?

- What situations make you feel defensive or reactive?

Going through these questions can help to establish where a lack of boundaries might come from, what your relationship to boundaries looks like, and areas in which your boundaries are not strict enough or do not exist at all. In order to identify what you need to feel safe and comfortable, refer back to your personal core values. You should also think about other scenarios that make you feel uncomfortable, stressed, depressed, or frustrated, writing them out as a list on a piece of paper.

How do I set my boundaries safely?

Once you have answered these questions and have written out your list of uncomfortable scenarios, let's set some boundaries. This is an ongoing process and you can always keep adding to the list.

Take a sheet of A4 paper and divide the page into two columns. On the left, write all of the situations and scenarios that lack boundaries. On the right, create a new boundary. To help with phrasing, here are a few examples what a boundary statement might look like:

- People may not ___________________

- I have the right to ask for ___________________

- To protect my energy and myself it is OK for me to ___________________

- To prevent stress/overwhelm/anxiety/depression/anger I need ___________________

Once we have identified these boundaries, we have to communicate them to others. The best case scenario is that we do so before our boundaries are even crossed. Unfortunately in many cases we only find out that we are lacking a boundary, or that it needs to be tighter, because it was crossed in the first place.

We want to make sure that our needs are well received and that we are not causing any harm with our words. The best way to be kind but firm is to use "I statements." I use Marshall B. Rosenberg's nonviolent communication framework (NVC) for this, too. NVC offers a great guideline for how to be very honest without doing any harm in the form of harsh criticism, insults, or put-downs.

These "I statements" look like this:

When I (see, hear, imagine…) ___________________ I feel ___________________ because I

need/value ___________________.

The NVC method outlines a 4th blank space, which is a request in the form of a question, such as, "Would you be willing to ______?". However, the goal of a boundary is to set a rule, limit, or guideline. In that case, a better version of this formula would be:

What I need is ________________________________.

To tie it together a little smoother, the full statement of boundaries could look like this:

I feel _____ when _____ because ____________________.

What I need is ________________________________.

As an example, setting a boundary with a partner could look like this:

I feel violated when you read the messages I exchange with my friends without asking me because I value privacy. What I need is a space that I know is private for conversations with my friends.

Don't forget that everyone is entitled to set their own rules, limits, and guidelines. Your boundaries will be laid out in a way that is comfortable and helpful for you, but that doesn't mean that the same set of rules apply to every person you meet.

It is a negotiation process. Your boundaries can change with every person you meet, and that is totally fine. You may feel comfortable hugging your lady friends but you don't want to hug your guy friends, for example. Maybe you are more at ease talking about money with your entrepreneurial friends but not with your family. This is all up to you and suspect to change at any time. Boundaries are flexible, and that's the beauty of them. We are allowed to have very different relationships with many different people, if we want to.

But how do we know what the other person's boundaries are? If they haven't been up front about them with you, you can always take the lead and ask. Asking how to make someone comfortable is a gift. As you get to know someone, you can ask them about their preferences in the scenarios you yourself have boundaries set for, or you can ask them when the situation comes up. For example, when greeting someone, you can ask "Hi, would you like a hug, or would you prefer a handshake?" Giving options is always a great way to ask for boundaries, since the other person can simply choose between one or the other, rather than having to say "No" which doesn't come easy for many people. You can also ask, "What is your favorite way to greet someone?" and let them tell you. If they tell you that they love to hug deeply and kiss people on the mouth and an alarm goes off in your head because this would cross your own boundary, you can respond with your own preferences and set a boundary in that way. For example, "Oh, that's a great way to say hello. I love to just keep it at a firm handshake!"

Understanding how to identify and safely set boundaries will help you to keep your energy levels high and prevent others from disrupting your mental space. Having a clear set of rules outlined for everyone to follow will also help you take ownership of your emotions and your interactions with others at all times.

2| CREATING HIGH STANDARDS & HOLDING YOURSELF TO THEM

"Wow, you are so difficult. You have such high standards!" I have heard this sentence all my life. And while my standards changed over time, my answer to this sentence only changed slightly. Ten years ago I would have said, "Well, maybe yours are just so low you can barely see them." , Today my response is, "Oh, yeah? Wow, thank you!"

Having high standards is powerful. Unless you don't hold yourself to them or make it a perfectionist competition to achieve them. High standards are amazing for filtering out people that you do not want to surround yourself with and experiences that would suck energy out of you. Overall, having high standards gives you a higher quality of life. .

"But what about being so difficult?" I'll tell you what. You are only difficult for people who do not have high standards for themselves, and people who are okay with being average and living a mediocre life. Harsh? Maybe. The truth? Yes.

Remember, standards are a quality indicator. Having no standards means there is a low quality level in this area of life. If someone says they are super easy-going and don't have high standards, I smile and wave and back out of the room. You can be easy-going and still have high standards. That's up to you.

But what does "having high standards" even look like?

Well, first I'm gonna share a few of the standards that I was holding onto ten years ago like the last donut in the box:

- Always be on time (translated from German, this means, "be at the meeting point 15 minutes early")

- Always be happy/positive (fake happiness alarm)

- Always get all of your work done before you go home (can you see what changed?)

Not only did I hold myself to these standards, I expected everyone I interacted with to fulfill them, too. That was ridiculous, especially when it came to the happiness part. It wasn't so much the expectation that you are not "allowed" to be sad or angry or depressed. But I expected people to bounce back super fast from it. After all, I did too, and I had all of these crazy traumas and challenges, right? So why couldn't you do it, too?

In hindsight, not only is that very cringe-worthy, but it also shows how much I censored myself by suppressing emotions and pretending to always be okay. That surely took a toll on me, and I had to work through much more for much longer than it would have taken me had I not held myself to these "standards" in the first place. Lesson learned.

Today, some of my high standards look like this:

- Always be kind (not "nice." Please don't be nice. Be kind.)

- Always speak your truth

- Use your privilege to create social change / impact

- Always keep your energy high (this is possible even when one is sad or going through a rough time)

- Always take care of yourself and love yourself first, and do it hard

- Do everything out of love, not out of fear

I have a lot of other standards. The list is long. Many of the standards that I hold myself to, I hold my friends and family to as well.

Having shared some of mine, let's look at how you can define yours. As you can see, you have no business holding others to standards that you won't hold yourself up to. That's not how it works. If you expect everyone to always be on time, but you are the one showing up late, this just looks like a badly-played power move. Ain't nobody got time to wait for you. If you want people to roll out the red carpet for you but you don't treat them the same way, you better pay someone to follow you around and do so.

Having said that, the best way I found to define my standards is to make a list with 3 columns, and put the three following questions at the top of each of them:

- What do you expect others to do/how do you expect others to behave in regular interactions with you? — List these expectations, one per row, in the first column.

- Would you do these things yourself without being asked? — Answer yes/no in the second column.

- Is that a non-negotiable behavior or expectation for you? — Answer yes/no in the third column

The expectations that made it through with 'Yes' in both columns 2 and 3 are things that you can put on your "High Standards List."

We could also filter this exercise for different kinds of relationships (for example, for your family, inner friend circle, partner, colleagues, acquaintances, etc.) and make a different list for each. You may have higher standards for your partner than you have for an acquaintance.

When you set your standards, you must hold yourself to them. That means to live and breathe these standards day in and day out. Does that mean you can never fail to achieve them? No. When I left Germany behind and spent my first two full years overseas, I slowly developed the tendency to not be "on time" anymore. I wasn't gonna be 15 minutes ahead of time for a meeting anymore. Instead I arrived exactly on time, and sometimes even 2 or 3 minutes late. When I visited Germany again for the first time after two and a half years, I wasn't used to the constant rush and "time is money" mentality anymore. I was 3 minutes late here and there and, I kid you not, 9 out of 10 times my friends called me (sometimes even 5 minutes ahead of time) to ask where I was. They knew me and my "always be on time" standards. It took me a few meetings to realize that this wasn't me anymore. I simply wasn't gonna be at a meeting point 15 minutes early anymore, wasting my time waiting for someone just so I could say, "I was here 15 minutes early." I had to set new expectations and inform my friends that in fact I had changed my standards. Their reaction: loud laughter. Some even said they didn't believe me when I told them that from now on I will either be on time or 2 or 3 minutes late. They laughed so hard I almost didn't take myself seriously. And then I was 2 minutes late. Oops. I guess I stopped living and breathing this standard. Slowly but surely, my friends believed me… although some did ask me if I had waited somewhere nearby for 20 minutes just so I could walk in 3 minutes late. This sounded like a lot of fun, but no. I simply wasn't on German time anymore. I had completely let go of that standard.

3| SETTING & MANAGING EXPECTATIONS

It's absolutely okay to change standards and adjust boundaries. What's important is communicating where we are at. Communicating boundaries and standards is just as important as setting expectations, and the two processes go hand in hand.

Setting and managing expectations comes in handy when working with clients. I love being very clear in my language and contracts about what my clients and their teams can expect from me, in what form it will be delivered, and by what dates or in what rhythm. There is nothing more powerful than setting up clear expectations for both sides as well as managing expectations that may come up during the first encounter or in the onboarding phase.

If I am not going to fulfill any of my clients' expectations, then I haven't done my job properly by setting and managing these in the beginning of our relationship. The same is true for all interpersonal relationships. I wish I was as clear and upfront with expectations in friendships as I am at work, but I am getting there.

Fear of rejection makes it hard for us to set expectations in any situation. When we set expectations, the other person always has the option to say, "No, that's not how I want to handle things." We tend to believe that if we entangle them in a commitment to the friendship/partnership/contract/etc., we can slowly engage them in our standards and boundaries and make them fulfil our expectations. That's not how it works. This is called manipulation.

A prime example of this sneaky strategy is getting into a relationship and wanting them to change "only this one thing." That "one thing" then usually turns into another 2 or 12 things. Spoiler alert: that doesn't work either.

Instead, we need to be upfront with our expectations and be willing to accept the risk that the other person will walk away. You should also be willing to walk away yourself, should the other person's expectations not match yours.

Unlike with boundaries and standards, I believe that expectations can be negotiated. If you live with your partner and they expect you to cook every night, which is an expectation that you do not share, you can negotiate a compromise. If your expectation is that your new friend never lies to you, which is one of your own standards, and your friend says they will try but can't promise it, then you can decide whether you stay and hope for the best or if you leave knowing you can't be friends with someone who may not always be honest with you.

The earlier you set the expectations in any relationship, the less you will have to manage them down the road. But what is the best way to communicate expectations? I am gonna be honest, if someone came up to me and told me, "I expect you to do this and be like that," I'd surely smile, say thanks for the warning, and walk away. No one (at least no high achiever that I know) likes to be told what to do. Instead, we can use the following samples and structures to express our expectations more politely.

For Business

I like to simply explain how I do my work, what I do, when I will deliver, and what results look like on average. Before signing the contract, I also walk my soon-to-be clients through processes, the systems I use, how often they will have access to me, what to expect in regard to different time zones, and more. I walk them through all of the pieces that belong to our shared work and ask after each step whether that is okay for them or if they have questions.

This is all the work of setting expectations. I don't leave anything up in the air. I explain payment structures, deadlines, and penalties for late payment. 90% of what I explain is non-negotiable. And because I make everything so clear and easy to understand, it is a very easy yes or no for the person talking to me.

If you want to set expectations with your team, it is important to explain what the expectation is (shared value/task/behavior/regular meeting attendance, etc.), how it will look when put into action, and whether there are any deadlines connected to it.

For Friendships/Partnerships/Family

Since you are not making a contract with your friends (at least I haven't heard of anyone doing so), running a soon-to-be friend through expectations you have may not sit well. It can be awkward to explain how you choose to operate your life when you don't even know where you are heading with this particular person. Instead, you can pick your top three expectations and phrase them with "I statements."

This method is also valid for family members and romantic partnerships, whether they are newly formed or already well-established. "I statements" help to set clear expectations without sounding demanding or straight-up demeaning.

These may be some helpful starters:

I love to do things this _______ and that_______way

I highly value _________________

I need _______________ so I can _______________

In a (partnership/friendship/roommate situation, etc.) I wish that _________________

My family would probably tell you that a few years ago I was definitely not patient enough to communicate this way. I would simply say "I expect _________from you." I have achieved what I intended a mere 10% of the time when communicating this way, and a solid 90% of the time I ran into a wall of resistance. There are only a few rare cases where it was actually necessary to be so extremely assertive, and that was when boundaries had been crossed and I needed to draw a clear line in the sand.

When we use nonviolent communication early on, we will be able to achieve our intended outcomes faster, prevent countless complications, and save a lot of energy, which is our ultimate goal.

SECTION 3| Breaking Patterns: Habits & Routines

Our goal is still to create an abundance of time. Throughout the book we have ventured out into many different areas that may not have seemed, at first, like they had much to do with time, but this is an obvious one.

Habits and routines are a big part of human nature. They assist our brain with tasks, decisions, and other processes that our brain runs on a daily basis. We don't have unlimited brain mass for all of these procedures, so our brain has to choose which ones to prioritize. Building habits and routines for tasks that are repeated regularly saves space and prevents overwhelm.

Let's have a look at what these words mean so we know how to use them properly.

Habits are actions and non-actions that are automatically executed based on a trigger. A habit is built of 3 steps: a trigger, the action or non-action, and a reward. These 3 steps together are also called a habit loop. Once this loop is repeated often enough it can become automated by the brain.

Routines are a set of habits, often created for a specific outcome. Morning and evening routines are very popular for entrepreneurs and high achievers and usually consist of different forms of mental, physical, spiritual, and emotional practices to help strengthen the body-mind-spirit connection.

Habit Stacks are a combination of habits that you perform as a chain reaction. Habit stacks are triggered by a single habit that is already implemented, automated, and performed on a subconscious level. These are most likely to be habits that you picked up in your childhood, like brushing your teeth. The stack consists of 3 or more habits and helps to immediately promote consistency with new habits.

The difference between a routine and a habit stack is that a routine is independent of any previously established habits.

Habit-making behaviors take place in the "basal ganglia" part of our brains, which is also responsible for emotional development, memories, and pattern recognition. Just imagine it sitting right in the middle of our brains. When a behavior that we repeat regularly starts to be automated by our brain, which means that it is turned into a habit, the decision-making part of the brain, the prefrontal cortex, goes into "sleep mode." The prefrontal cortex is the part of our brain that sits right behind our forehead, and it is also associated with storing information as well as decision-making.

Our brain wants to build as many habits as possible so that it can free up as much brain mass as possible to use for highly important decisions, strategic thinking, and all of the non-habitual tasks we are busy with.

How long does it take to build a habit?

That's probably a scientist's favorite question. And mine. My clients used to ask me about the 21-day rule that so many blog posts and articles suggested for years and years. My answer was always, "If you are not willing to do it longer than 21 days, why even start?" The reality is that, no matter what habit you build, you still gotta do it. Even though your brain automates it somewhat, you still can't opt out of the experience. How would you like to implement the habit of eating healthy, fresh, non-processed food daily, but after 21 days end up at fast food restaurants again? That doesn't work. And although there is definitely a difference between the effort required when you first start out building a new habit and what's needed to execute that behavior years after the habit is already built, you are still the one executing it.

That said, there are indeed indicators for how long it can take to start a new behavior, automate it, and form a habit out of it. Phillippa Lally, a scientist in health psychology at University College London, has found that it takes anywhere between 18 and 254 days to form a new habit. The data from this study suggests that it takes an average of 66 days of regularly performing and repeating new behavior in order to automate it into a habit.

Are all habits helpful habits?

We take on many habits accidentally, like smoking cigarettes in times of stress. These can be coping mechanisms, habits we modelled from our parents or other authority figures, or habits formed out of boredom. Remember, our brain does not like to be bored, and it will always look for something to be busy with. Smoking cigarettes is one way to do so. Not a very healthy one, in my books, but no judgement over here. I myself smoked for some time to deal with stress in my corporate years.

I would define healthy habits as habits that help us to achieve a certain goal, produce a certain outcome, or support our life in a positive way. We want to implement as many healthy habits as necessary to create the best possible outcome for our automated behaviors. These habits can change over time depending on our goals and desired outcomes.

In contrast to this, unhealthy habits are the ones we adopted consciously or unconsciously that don't serve our goals anymore. These could be anything from outdated coping mechanisms to fitness regimes or the time that you go to bed. If it doesn't serve you and your goals anymore, change it.

How do I break habits?

Our brain loves structure and repetition, so habits are best formed in a stable environment. The flip side of this is that breaking habits works best when you change your environment. This could be on vacation, during a business trip, or even during a different time and place of your day.

When I work with my clients we combine the process of breaking a habit with the formation of a new one. If you break an old habit without forming a new, healthy one at the same time, you'll leave an empty space in your brain, which creates a sense of boredom that often translates to craving the exact thing you want to leave behind.

For example: Quitting sugar (or any products that include processed, flavored, or added sugars)

Instead of just quitting all processed sugars, we will replace this unhealthy eating habit with a healthy one. Every time we crave any kind of processed sugar (other than fresh fruit for example) we will drink a glass of filtered water instead. This helps you to not only quit an unhealthy habit but to form a new, healthy one at the same time.

The best time to make this change is when you are in a different, less familiar location. If you happen to be traveling soon after making the decision to quit sugar, wait for the trip to get started. If you don't travel, then make a location change in your daily life. If your old habit was to buy a donut on the way to your office, then change the location and buy a healthy snack at a different shop instead.

We often get hung up on the little details, like not knowing which products we can eat and what kind of sugar is okay to consume. In that case, we will start with research. Prepare a list of products that you can eat and that you like to eat, as well as restaurants that cook without added sugar.

From there, you can set yourself a reminder in your phone, depending on the new habit, that keeps reminding you throughout the day not to go back to the old habit. There are also habit-tracking apps out there which include many great additional functions to support your new behaviors.

In short:

- Change location or your typical rhythm to break a habit more easily

- Prepare all necessary information, possible equipment, etc. ahead of time to help reduce obstacles

- Replace an old habit with a new one to stop craving the old one

- Set reminders for the new habit

How do I create a routine?

I mentioned morning and evening routines before. Building these will differ in terms of elements to include simply because the outcome is different for both of them.

To create an efficient and well-working morning routine, it is best to include 4 different elements:

1. Physical Activity

2. Mental Training

3. Spiritual Practise

4. Emotional Exercise

Physical Activities will not only increase your energy but also your overall health. I am not talking about hours of hard exercise. This is up to you. Maybe you like to go to the gym and follow a set of workouts each morning in order to achieve a certain body goal. What I mean, though, is movement. Any kind of exercise, movement, or stretching that helps your body unblock and move energy, relaxes your muscles, and gets the oxygen flow going.

You could do yoga on a paddleboard in the pool, swim with sharks, or do jumping jacks at the supermarket cashier. I am sure the people around you would love it, too. If none of those are for you, then you can go with more conventional exercise like taking a walk in the park, dancing around at home, or even just a 10-minute pushup and burpee sprint. The most important thing is that you move your whole body. Whether it is slow or fast doesn't matter. The intention and the actual movements are what count.

Natural sunlight is an absolute must for our bodies, especially in the morning, for many reasons. Sunlight boosts serotonin (the "happiness" neurotransmitter) and helps regulate cholesterol and melatonin so that we can produce plenty of Vitamin D and sleep well later at night. So when you get up in the morning to move, try your best to go outside and take some deep breaths of fresh air while you're at it.

Mental Training will keep your brain fit and up-to-date. If you want to master a skill, learn a new language, or add some new knowledge to your extensive "database" then the morning is a great time to do so.

Learn something new, take a course, listen to a podcast or audiobook. Practice your new skill, speak the new language. Learning something in the morning actually sticks faster, since your brain has gotten rid of toxins and waste and pruned unnecessary information the night before. The first 4 hours after waking up are the very best time to add knowledge or continue with mastering a skill, so why not add this to your morning routine?

Even 20 minutes each day can make a huge difference. Just 20 minutes a day is still 20 minutes more than 99% of the other people out there. And that's what sets you apart.

Spiritual Practice brings our mind, body, and spirit in alignment. This sounds more "woo" than it really is because spiritual practice is what helps us become more resilient for the rough times.

Some common spiritual practices for high achievers include body scanning, any meditation practice, reiki, energy clearing, or simply being silent and present with yourself. You can also go all the way woo and work with oracle cards and crystals and ask your spirit guides for help.

If none of these quite appeal to you, simply listen to the voice inside and focus on what you are most grateful for in this moment. Then write 3 to 5 of these things down and keep them in a gratitude journal.

Whatever you decide to do, and whatever is YOUR way to do it, activating our spirit and setting positive and impactful intentions for the day is what will move you forward fast. It doesn't matter what religion you follow or if you follow one at all. You can use your own religious practises as spiritual practices, too. The important part is bringing the body, mind, spirit into alignment.

Emotional Exercises are the ones that strengthen your EQ (emotional intelligence quotient). Why do we want that? Well there are hundreds of reasons really, but the most important is for the sake of your peace of mind, peace of heart, and peace of spirit. Having a high EQ means that you can control your emotions (which are very different from suppressing them), accept them, and move through them without holding on to them.

There are specific exercises to release stuck emotions. Energy body work. Crying, laughing, screaming, being goofy and connecting with your heart and soul. You can do specific therapies or go through specific coaching programs. Other amazing methods that can help you strengthen your EQ are breathwork exercises or taking ice baths (after Wim Hof) which also support your mindset and immune system.

With these four elements—physical activity, mental training, spiritual practice, and emotional exercise—you can now set up your very own morning routine that fits your lifestyle and helps you reach your personal goals.

HABITS & ROUTINES

www.moniquelindner.com @themoniquelindner

But what about the evening routine? We don't want to go to bed like a squirrel on ecstasy so what can we do to calm the mind, the body, and the spirit down and prepare for a restful night of sleep? The following are my favorite evening routines:

Decreasing artificial and blue lights a minimum of 1 to 2 hours before bed helps our brain to slow down and shut off any hyperactivity. That means turning off any screens (yes, including your phone, computer, kindle, TV, and all other kinds of screens) as well as any light sources that are not natural or warm. As our brain goes through its nightly detox process, all of the information that has been newly added or was repeated often will be processed, while information that hasn't been used often or recently will go into the bin. This means that if you watch TV before bed, chances are high that your brain will process that information while you sleep. Personally, I have yet to find a program on TV that I would like to remember.

Meditating and writing in a gratitude journal before bed instead will help you keep everything that you are grateful for at the front and center of your memory and help keep your energy high. You can visualize your life, meditate on your achievements so far, or simply do a body scan to move into a calm end of the day.

Sound baths are an amazing healing and relaxation modality and I personally use these every night to go to sleep. There are many different versions and also different purposes that each method is used for. I like to listen to one that is created with Tibetan singing bowls and specifically aims to relax the body and the mind for better sleep.

Taking a warm shower before bed will do wonders. Sleep hygiene is not often spoken about, yet it has a huge effect on our sleep. I shower cold in the morning to start the day and get the blood flow going and warm at night to relax the muscles and calm my brain down. There is a whole lot to say about changing environments, showering, changing clothes, and making a clean physical cut with a cue of triggers for your mind to distinguish between "this was my life during the day" and "now it's night time." But that would explode the book even more, so just know that you can research more about it, and I am quite sure I will write about it on my website soon enough (if I haven't done so already).

The intention of morning and evening routines is the same: to bring your mind, body, and spirit into alignment and prepare for the upcoming part of the day, or night.

SECTION 4| The Power of Focus

Setting an intention for your day or night with your individual routine gives you the best possible foundation to focus on what is really important. That may be your most important task of the day, a team meeting, being present with your partner, or having an amazing joyful day off without thinking about work.

Focus is what will get you to achieve the big, audacious goals in your life, whatever they are. What does it look like to truly focus?

To focus is to channel our attention on one central point of interest for a specific time frame. That time frame can be 90 minutes, it can be 5 weeks, or it can be 7 months. For many people it is extremely difficult to focus on one single activity for an extended amount of time. For others it is the key to unlocking flow state. With that being said, there are a few cornerstones that will help you to stay more focused, whether it is for just one task, a fun activity, or a project that you would like to complete.

The Myth of Multitasking

Our brain is not made to multitask. Sure, you can cook dinner and watch TV at the same time, and you can write an email while listening to music. But you are not really concentrating on both of these tasks simultaneously.

Although you feel like you are getting more things done, the opposite is actually true. Our brain can not focus on two tasks at the same time. Thus, you are really only concentrating on one of the tasks while the other is running on autopilot in the background.

When attempting to multitask, our brain is constantly switching back and forth between the tasks we are trying to do simultaneously. Our brain needs an average of 10-40 minutes to reach full concentration on a new task, which means that when multitasking, we can never actually focus on any of the tasks fully. Unless you want both of these tasks to be half-done, which also results in a lack of quality, you definitely want to stop multitasking.

This is why the number one principle to follow is: **If you want to get more done, you need to do less. Preferably one thing at a time.**

Distractions are dream-killers

And there you go. Just a minute ago you wanted to research somet... and then you saw a squirrel. This squirrel!

Did you know that the human attention span is lower than that of a goldfish? Yep. The goldfish has an attention span of 9 seconds, 2 seconds longer than we humans do. Not kidding. To be able to stay laser-focused for the time of our work we must put some effort in.

Silence your phone, social media, and any devices with noticeable notifications. This may sound obvious, but many people underestimate the impact of notifications, whether they are sounds, vibrations, pop-ups, or even just light. I started to silence all of my devices in 2011 when I took a job in the Digital Transformation Agency back in Berlin. Since social media channels were part of our daily work with clients, I often received hundreds of notifications, updates, and emails on top of my private ones. It took me a week to decide this would drive me insane. I turned them all off. On all devices, whether for work or my personal ones. I enjoyed being able to take a break from being available if I needed to, so I kept all notifications turned off, and they have remained that way until this day. I also don't have any ringtones for my phone—no vibrations, nothing. If I don't know ahead of time that you are going to call me, I won't answer the phone anyway. This is pretty radical, and for other people this may not work as well as it does for me. But reducing all audible and visible outputs of notifications will make a huge difference for your focus, as it will not interrupt your brain with a distraction each time one pops up.

Locking your phone away completely in random places while you are working on your most important tasks will help to take a lot of distractions off your plate. You may have heard the saying "out of sight, out of mind," and it is very accurate. Although it takes longer for your desire for the distraction to be decreased, it can help to simply place your phone in random places that you usually would not place it and get to work. A study has shown that "if a person is aware of a substitute for something, the longer they have gone without, the weaker their desire for the non-consumed good becomes." In other words, if you put the phone away and substitute the craving for using it with working on an important task, you will soon forget about the phone, at least for an extended amount of time.

I put my phone in a different spot every day so it won't become a habit for my brain to know where it is and want to go look if there are any updates or messages.

Blocking all social media apps and browser access on your computer will further reduce any distractions. Since our brain is a smart little machine up there, it will try to find any other way to access all of the information that it would usually have access to on our phones. Shiny objects are soooooo… shiny! And our brain wants them all! So we gotta protect it from them.

There are many browser extensions and apps available, both for your computer and for your phone that can block you from browsing the internet or checking social media for the time you choose to work. To gamify this and get some virtual rewards, the app "forest" on your phone lets you plant lovely trees and build, well, forests.

Being hungry or thirsty is a great reason to be distracted. I always have a big bottle of water on my desk, plus some healthy snacks like nuts or seeds or veggie sticks. Staying properly hydrated helps your brain perform at high levels, and although it certainly is very healthy to get up and stretch at least once every hour, having to fill up your water glass more often than that can become a distraction.

These are just 4 out of hundreds of scenarios that we could walk through in order to help you reduce distractions and increase your focus. Yet there are other methods that will certainly be more effective in the long run, like working within your preferred productivity type that I explained at the very beginning of this book.

Finally, I want to explain one last method that helped me build up the ability to focus on one single task for an extended period of time.

Learn how to refocus

While it is great to prevent distractions from the get-go, it is just as important to know how to get back to focus as fast as possible after being distracted.

Sometimes it is actually helpful to take a step back, allow yourself to be distracted for a short while, and then step back into the task with fresher eyes. Think about a camera that focuses on one spot taking photos. When something in the background moves or changes, the focus may change too. We have to adjust the lens to get back to our focal point.

The same is valid for our work. When writing this book I had days where I would have nothing else but writing planned. I would write for stretches of 2.5 hours without a break for a total of 7 to 9 hours. To be able to stay focused and on-topic, I would periodically look up from the screen for a few seconds, look out into the trees, and then go back to writing.

Sometimes I would encounter different thoughts and the urge to research topics further, even if there was no need to do so. My brain would start thinking about what other information I could put in the book besides what I had already been writing about, and I would get distracted by these thoughts. Sometimes I would think for too long about what I wanted to eat for dinner when it was only 10 a.m. To be able to get back to writing quickly, I would use the same trick.

I would look up, interrupt both my writing and my thoughts, and look out into the trees. This works with anything that doesn't trigger specific thoughts for you. You can look outside of the window, at a photo, or you can also get up and stretch. The point is to interrupt the train of thought that is keeping you distracted. As soon you have interrupted that pattern, say the task that you were working on out loud and remind yourself what steps you have to take action on in order to fulfill the task. Refocus and get back to work.

For some people, it is helpful to be distracted in between tasks or during a longer stretch of work. In this case, I recommend scheduling distraction times. I had clients who, in trying to avoid distractions completely, ended up creating so much FOMO around not checking their phones that they weren't able to concentrate on their tasks at all.

Instead of waiting for the distraction to arise, plan it out. If you are one of the productivity types that works in shorter time frames, then schedule yourself some short sprints of distraction, for example a 5-minute social media break after 2 work sessions, or a 5-minute blog post break after 4 sessions. Whatever feels right to you and helps you to stay more focused when you are actually working on your tasks.

The power of focus lies not in ginormous stretches of uninterrupted work (although achievable), nor in unlocking some secret area of the brain, but in a very realistic approach. All it takes is reducing distractions to the best of your abilities, preventing cravings for shiny objects, assessing your productivity type, and learning how to quickly and effectively refocus.

SECTION 5| Intuition: Trust That You Know

If someone were to ask me today what the biggest energy vampires of my life have been so far, I would tell them, "toxic people and not trusting my intuition." We spoke about toxic people already, so let's talk about intuition. Since we are about to wrap this book up, I feel like this is the perfect topic to do so.

Intuition is the ability to instinctively know or understand a situation, incident, or something else without the need to verify any data, validate any facts, or consult conscious reasoning. It is your sixth sense or gut feeling. Over time, trusting our intuition helps strengthen it, as it is reinforced by the decisions we make, as well as by our experiences and memories.

We are all born with the ability to tap into our intuition, yet many of us never learn to trust it. Why is that? As with everything we learn in life that is not an instinct, the first 7 to 10 years of a child's development are the most influential.

As we grow we learn by listening, modeling, and trial and error. Often, we are corrected. "Don't do that." "No, that's not how you do it." Children who are not given space to explore their own ways of doing things often suppress their intuition because they are told that listening to their intuition will be "wrong" or not result in a desirable outcome. So they don't follow their intuition and instead do whatever they are told.

This is a never-ending story. I remember when I was growing up as a girl, there was always something I was doing wrong, even when I wasn't doing anything. That was wrong, too. Not just at home but in school, around friends, at ballet school, and certainly when I was with extended family. There wasn't much you could do "right." There were just too many opinions available to keep everyone satisfied.

Over time, I learned not to trust myself. Every time my intuition showed up, I fought it. My brain went into overdrive, weighing in on every scenario, constantly trying to find the "safest" and most "pleasing" of them all. Sure enough, that didn't work either. What it did do was suck the energy out of me like a vampire.

Not listening to my intuition got me into twice as much trouble than following it ever could have.

I had to unlearn the fight against my greatest tool.

It started with my second burnout in 2011 when my life turned upside down… again. This second round came in a matter of 5 years, but this one was more painful on all levels. Physically, emotionally, spiritually, I was devastated. But there was no way for me to take a break or give up. I promise, though, there were plenty of days that I wished I wasn't such a high achiever and could just let it be.

But that was never me, fortunately. One day, when I was all but immobilized from my spine injury, I hesitated before taking the dose of morphine I was given each day. My doctor has prescribed the highest possible dose of morphine for me to take at home throughout the day, yet it didn't help release any of the pain. The only effect it had was that I had almost completely lost control of my body, my mind faster than a German race car and my thoughts endlessly negative. I suddenly had this weird feeling that I shouldn't take these meds anymore, that they made me more sick than helping me. I had already been taking them for more than 4 months and I had to get the pain under control. I was about to start a new job, hopefully. Yet I didn't feel like showing up like this. My intuition said I should stop taking them, but from a medical standpoint I knew I couldn't just take my body off of them cold turkey.

That was the first day I trusted myself, my body, and my needs, even though it was sure to be a painful ride. For a few days, I stopped taking the morphine. I went back to my doctor to ask for a healthy way to detox my body from the medication and to find alternative pain relief.

I would never recommend that anyone just throw away their medication or stop taking it. In this case, it was extremely important for me to trust that I would be okay and that this decision was right for me. But more importantly, it wasn't really about the medication, but about learning that my intuition was there and that following it would support me on my journey.

Unlearning the Untruths

To be able to trust myself and my intuition again, I first had to start unlearning everything about myself that didn't feel true to me. Things that people would say out of fear, judgement, jealousy, or whatever other reason. Things that I had started to believe myself but were simply not true. Things that interfered heavily with my ability to trust myself. For example:

Noone would ever want to love someone like you. Nobody wants to be around people who are always so sick like you. You are a burden to everyone. People are only friends with you because they get something from you.

The greatest untruth of them all was that I came to believe *I was not worthy of being alive.*

Lies. Straight-up lies. Beliefs like this would not only prevent me from trusting myself, but also from asking for help even when I really needed it. I didn't trust anyone to be my friend just because I am awesome. I tried to please people as a full-time job that I was not a burden. All of it made life itself a pain in the ass.

I had to unlearn all of these kinds of beliefs. I started by rewriting new beliefs based on what I thought to be true about myself. Then I went out to prove them right. This sounds fairly simple but it certainly is not, especially with the cognitive biases our brain carries.

Success is a matter of repeating these new beliefs often, even just thinking about them. When you doubt yourself, stop as soon you recognize it and rewind back to the new beliefs. You have to detox the people that don't hold these positive beliefs about you or don't actually prove them to be true. And you have to change a lot of behavior surrounding how you show up for yourself and for others in line with these new beliefs.

There are so many more ways to change your beliefs, some of which we talked about previously in this book.

Tapping into your intuition

I had to learn and practice this for years (yes, I said years) after I unlearned the greatest untruth about myself, simply because it felt so risky. Having said that, now I wouldn't want to live a day without it anymore. Sometimes it is annoying how accurate my intuition is, but I won't complain.

There are quite a few things that I have done in order to call in my intuition again, and I want to share them with you.

Being in solitude was probably one of the biggest intuition aids for me then, and it still is today. Not only traveling solo but also just being by myself, and not being busy. No phone, no books, no podcasts, nothing to keep my mind occupied. Just being present with myself and listening. That is not always comfortable, and for some it may sound scary, but being able to just be with yourself, listening to your thoughts and letting them pass, is extremely powerful.

At some point—it could be minutes, hours, or days—the cloud in your mind will dissolve and whatever you were looking for will appear. This could be a feeling. It could be a random thought that pops up and seems to be completely unrelated but shows you a solution or a new way. It could be a sign that you suddenly see all around you. Whatever it is, it will come up.

Listen. Once that intuition pops up in whatever way it does, listen to it. Don't push it away. Don't put it off. Don't dismiss it as some weird or random thing. Don't talk yourself out of it. Listen. Write it out. Do not overthink it. Just take action on it.

Feel it in your body. This one has been huge for me. I can only guess that because of both my many physical struggles as well as my training as a ballerina I have always been very aware of my body. I listened to it even more closely after my spine injury. This means that I have been able to identify exactly what fear and worry feels like in my body, what excitement feels like, where my intuition shows up, what my body does when toxicity shows up around me, and so on. I have developed quite an acute alarm system for all of it, and I appreciate it a lot even though it can be painful at times.

Trust that when something feels off, it probably is. I promise you, it's better to be wrong about trusting that feeling than ignore it and run into trouble instead. In hindsight, I have missed quite a few signs, which meant I had to learn the lesson the hard way. Which I surely did. Now I listen closely and if something feels off, even if I don't know why, even if it's not something I can explain, I walk away. I'd rather walk away too often than not enough.

Be aware of your surroundings. I see so many people walking along the road with their faces in their phone screens and I wonder how they make it safely to their destinations. Never mind the people who do that while driving a car or motorcycle. I am not even talking about the physical risk of running into a pole or driving into a wall. There are hundreds of other things that could happen just because you weren't aware. That's how the story of my phone being robbed out of my hands started and ended: with me walking on the side of the road looking at my screen. That was the last time I did that, and that was in 2012. We give the power of our intuition away simply by failing to be aware of our surroundings. This shouldn't be confused with being paranoid, however.

Keep a notebook of every time you trusted yourself and your intuition and great things happened. The next time your intuition pops up and you begin to doubt yourself, you have a powerful reminder that in fact, you can trust yourself.

Following your intuition and trusting yourself is the greatest gift you can give yourself. It will make you fall deeper in love with yourself, want to take better care of yourself and most of all, it will save yourself so much energy. Give it a try!

THAT'S A WRAP

Wow. Before I wrap this book up with some final words I want to say thank you!

Thank you to all the readers who trusted me and bought this book. I appreciate every single one of you.

Thank you to all of my clients who trusted me and my work and put all of the effort in to create such phenomenal results

Thank you to my sister and my parents for always supporting me in my journey, no matter how unconventional it looked or how far away from them it took me.

Thank you to Gahmya Drummond-Bey, my incredible writing coach, and all of our fellow authors and creators that took part in her writers' retreat. If it wasn't for all of you, this book wouldn't be in your hands now.

Thank you to Gregory Giagnocavo for planting the seed in my head that it is not only possible for me to write a book during a pandemic but that I absolutely must put my knowledge out there.

Thank you to my incredible editor Tyler Rose Mann, who not only kept me humble and sane throughout this whole journey but who I was able to fully trust and put this piece of art in her hands without worrying that it would come out worse than when I gave it to her. Letting go of control is still a practice and wow has that been an amazing one for me and a wonderful experience seeing how Tyler has honored it. THANK YOU.

Thank you Universe for never letting me down.

You know, writing this book was almost like the last bit of proof to myself that everything in here is true. It is my truth, and maybe soon it will be yours.

But maybe you have arrived here and are wondering: How have I created an abundance of time now? And that's the last question I'd love to answer and close this book out with.

The honest answer is probably: You won't.

And that is not because I was lying or clickbaiting the title, but simply because this is a lifelong work of implementation.

What I know to be true is that we can not manage our time nor control it. But we can manage our energy, we can lead our life with intention, we can keep our mind focused and use our time wisely.

I know for the first 19 years of my life I didn't and I was lucky enough to get a wake-up call. Or two. Maybe that wasn't luck. Maybe I was chosen to go through this to be here now and tell you my story, share my experiences, and urge you to create a limitless life for yourself.

All of what you just read is one step per page towards a limitless life. I have walked them all, I live them daily. Even when I fail a day or two, I pick up the pace right after.

I want you to have a limitless life, too. One with an abundance of time.

This is my work to help you do so.

Just remember, as my granddad said:

"You can do anything and be anyone you want in your life!"

And as long as I knew him, he was always right.

AUTHOR BIOGRAPHY

Monique Lindner is a High Performance & Leadership specialist, TEDx speaker, and location-independent entrepreneur.

Her clients range from start-ups to Fortune 500 companies like Apple. She works with business leaders and CEOs and their teams of up to 160 people in helping them to optimize their efficiency, build solid leadership skills, improve their mindset, and create massive impact.

With her unique The T.I.M.E. Method® and her tagline 'Slow Down to Speed Up', she is on a mission to help business owners take back control of their time and energy and grow impactful businesses.

By integrating the 4 pillars of The T.I.M.E. Method®, Monique has helped her clients cut up to 50% of working hours while doubling and tripling their revenue. Her work also resulted in significantly reducing stress, anxiety, and overwhelm while building unbreakable confidence.

Monique has built her business with a complete location-independent infrastructure, traveled to 44 countries as well as lived and worked in 8 of them in management positions. This gives her unique insights into cross-cultural work ethics and has helped her build an incredible skill set of team culture development over the past 14 years while working abroad.

Monique has also survived & healed from two chronic diseases, sexual violence as well as other forms of abuse. She has spent years transforming trauma, adversity, and hardship into personal growth, and transforming her pain into power.

Today Monique is committed to combining all of her outstanding knowledge & experiences to unlock the ultimate potential of her clients!

www.moniquelindner.com

@themoniquelindner